On Wings of FAITH

On Wings of

FAITH

My Daily Walk
with a Prophet

Frederick Babbel

ISBN: 1-55517-354-3

10 9 8 7 6 5 4 3 2 1

Published and Distributed by:

925 North Main, Springville, UT 84663 • 801/489-4084

CFI   Publishing and
      Distribution Since 1986

Cedar Fort, Incorporated

CFI Distribution • CFI Books • Council Press • Bonneville Books

Cover design by Lyle Mortimer
Page layout by Corinne A. Bischoff
Printed in the United States of America

Contents

Preface

This book *had* to be written!

One afternoon when I was in President Henry D. Moyle's office, he said, "Brother Babbel, you must write a book about some of the faith-promoting things you heard and experienced in your mission to Europe." President George Albert Smith also inquired about it. President Hugh B. Brown reminded me that, as one of the two living witnesses (Elder Ezra Taft Benson and myself), I had an obligation to make this account available to others.

But mostly *On Wings of Faith* has been written because of the numerous people who have urged, after hearing my account, that these precious gems be published and so made accessible to them and their children.

Most of the items are taken from my daily journal, which was written under tremendous pressure with no attempt to achieve literary fluency.

On Wings of Faith recounts some of the most faithpromoting experiences in the history of God's dealing with his children during the twentieth century. It is a witness that the Lord's promise "...they shall go forth and *none shall stay them*, for I the Lord have commanded them" (Doctrine and Covenants 1:5) is a divine passport for his servants.

No one could live as the participants did during those eventful days, without knowing through the revelations of the Almighty that he lives, that he is all-powerful, that he blesses and sustains his servants. The age of miracles is *not* past! It is *always* present for those who live, believe, and obey.

These experiences have been of inestimable value to my family and our friends through the years. May they be of similar value to you and yours.

Acknowledgments

I express sincere gratitude to the late Don C. Corbett, who made some of his materials available and invited me to use whichever parts I wished.

I express appreciation also to the *Reader's Digest* for permission to include excerpts from a special article written for that magazine by Elder Ezra Taft Benson of the Council of the Twelve; and to the Progress Research Corporation for permission to include a brief excerpt concerning Dunkirk from their *Complete History of World War II,* by Francis Trevelyan Miller, Litt.D., LL.D.

Special thanks are due my devoted wife, who never flagged in her determination to see this book in final form, and to my children and sons-in-law who assisted with the selections, proofreading, and various helpful suggestions. My daughter, Julene Updike, undertook the actual final typing of the manuscript for publication, while her husband, Lisle, proofread all manuscripts and galley proofs. My artist friend John C. Craddock provided rough sketches for the jacket design.

Without the patience and painstaking editorial and other assistance of Marvin W. Wallin and George Bickerstaff of Bookcraft, however, this book would still not be available.

I appreciate the many friends who have been waiting patiently for this volume to be published.

Beyond all else, I express my deep gratitude for the privilege of participating in the memorable events this book records.

And the voice of warning shall be unto all people, by the mouths of my disciples, whom I have chosen in these last days.

And they shall go forth and none shall stay them, for I the Lord have commanded them.

— Doctrine and Covenants 1:4-5

chapter one

"None Shall Stay Them"

As the C-47 army transport plane nosed toward the steel landing strip I leaned from my canvas bucket seat to look out of the window. The flight from England had been uneventful. The sea around the Dutch coastline had looked calm and peaceful as the flat green landscape welcomed us with its cries-cross of canals and streams. I had work to do down there in Holland, the first country I was visiting on this special postwar mission.

Getting here at all had been accomplished only by a succession of seeming miracles. As the mind will, mine reviewed with split-second speed the events of the last six weeks: the phone calls from Elder Ezra T. Benson and President David O. McKay; the official mission call; my wife June's inspiring support; my securing an honorable discharge from the army three months before the due time; the further "impossible" achievement of obtaining my passport, visas to ten European countries, and special military permits to the four zones in Germany and Austria—all in two weeks; the special blessing I had received from the First Presidency. These and a hundred associated recollections flooded upon me as the green land of Holland rose up to meet the plane that February day of 1946.

The fairyland appearance of red-tiled roofs and luxuriant fields deceptively suggested to the air traveler an immunity from the effects of World War II, which had ended in Europe only nine months previously. When we landed, I learned better. Along the bus route from the airport to The Hague, the roads showed unmistakable evidence of bombing and strafing. The hurried repairs made resulted in a rough ride. Bomb blasts had robbed many houses of their windows, while in other lesser-damaged homes life appeared to be proceeding normally. The city proper was another matter. Entire blocks had been leveled to the ground, most of the rubble being still in evidence. The most desolate section was the area from which the Germans had launched V-2 rockets on England. The Allies had had to wipe out this entire section in self-defense. En route we were informed that the heart of Rotterdam was still nothing but a mass of twisted steel and debris.

When we arrived at the K.L.M. (Dutch Air Lines) office, I noticed three men examining a photograph and showing it to the pilot of our plane. I decided to investigate. It was President Ezra Taft Benson's picture. Having introduced myself, I learned that these men were Brother S. Schipaanboord, acting mission president, Brother Peter Vlam, his second counselor, and Brother Theodore Mebius, the mission president's son-in-law.

It was Elder Benson whose phone call from Salt Lake City to my San Francisco apartment on the previous New Year's Eve had set off the exciting chain of events which had brought me to Europe on a second mission for the Church. The First Presidency had called him to reestablish the European Missions following the long night of war, and to arrange for the distribution of such necessaries as food, clothing and bedding to the distressed saints in Europe. The thrilling assignment was mine to assist him in this great work.

We had flown out of Salt Lake City on January 29. Having set up our office in London, we had now separated for a few days. President Benson flew to Paris on February 11 to arrange for the purchase of automobiles for the use of mission presidents. He left two days later for Holland in company with LDS chaplain Howard C. Badger of the U.S. Army, whose services on this initial tour of Europe were to prove invaluable in facilitating contacts with army officials and others. My assignment was to book our transportation to Denmark, Norway and Sweden, make my way to Holland by whatever means I could, and meet Elder Benson there. Like the three men I had just met in The Hague, I was anxious to find the man who fitted their photograph.

In quick time the four of us inched our way into a small

German D.K.W. two-cylinder car and made our way to the mission president's home in Utrecht. During the time we were together I was told that, although many Dutch people understood and spoke German, they resented highly the indignity of having to do so during their recent occupation by German troops. The Germans had confiscated practically everything they could locate. Only those bicycles and cars which were completely dismantled and buried in the ground (except for those retained by the collaborators, whom the Dutch regarded with contempt) remained in the land. Even the car in which we were riding had been taken completely apart when the Germans came into Holland. Each part had been covered with cosmoline and carefully buried in the ground where it couldn't be found. When the war ended, the owners dug their machines out of the ground, removed the heavy grease in which they were wrapped, and put them back into service.

I learned that every able-bodied man the Nazis could capture had been used for some kind of slave labor. For 5 1/2 years most Dutch men tried to avoid arrest by living "underground," sustaining themselves on a very meager diet. Many were caught and executed, but the underground workers continued to resist— killing several Germans, where possible, for every one of their own number that had been captured and killed. Children were kidnapped and women were threatened to force fathers and husbands out of hiding. Murder and thievery as a means of reprisal had become common practices It was a time of sickening horror.

Along the highways were both broken and intact tank obstacles, barbed-wire entanglements, etc. Most of the bridges and their piling, had been bombed or dynamited. Railroad yards and wharfs had been blasted. For a time German river barges had even been transporting precious Dutch topsoil—reclaimed from the ocean bed through their famous system of dikes—into Germany, adding insult to injury.

In February 1946 everything was strictly rationed, although some items were obtainable on the "black market" at exorbitant prices. About a year previously, I was told, a pair of common wooden work shoes cost over $50.00. People had learned effectively to steal as a result of the war occupation years and continued this practice in the interests of self-survival. I was informed that if a person left his car unguarded for just an hour, he might expect to find it with its wheels removed as well as some of the working parts of the engine.

The few cars and bicycles to be seen on the streets were, for the most part, those which had remained buried in the ground until the German occupation forces had been removed. Most of the railroad rolling stock had been taken out of the country by the retreating Germans or had been destroyed during the war. These extreme shortages made traveling unpleasant and difficult. According to the manager of the hotel where I had secured rooms for President Benson and myself, there wasn't a single taxi in operation in The Hague at that time.

As appalling as were the scars of war, the moral decadence gave one an even more sickening impression. According to my traveling companions, honesty and trustworthiness seemed to have almost totally disappeared. Standards of sexual morality had reached a low point never known before in that country. Nearly all men and women—and even many small children— smoked. (This was true in England as well.) The habit seemed to be far more prevalent than in the United States.

In checking with the Dutch airline officials, I learned that the flight reservations I had made for us in London had been canceled and that we could nor expect to secure any plane reservations to Denmark for at least ten days. All my efforts failed to persuade them that we absolutely must leave in two days. They adamantly reminded me that travel space was extremely limited and was reserved only for the military and high governmental officials. There was no other means of transportation to Denmark at the present time, they told me. I knew these developments would be a keen disappointment for President Benson, but I saw no way around the problem.

President Benson failed to arrive at the American Embassy at the arrival time he had wired to them, but they handed me a telegram advising that he would arrive not by car as planned but by train in the late afternoon.

There were two railway stations at The Hague. When I checked at the Niederlaendische station, the station master told me that the train corresponding with the schedule I had been given was a small local shuttle-service and that any passengers from France or Belgium would have to arrive at the Staats station, which was located more than a mile from this station.

A through train from Paris was due to arrive at the Staats station in a few minutes, so I hurried over there on foot, running most of the way. President Benson was not aboard that train. The next train from France was due in about another hour, so I hurried back to the Niederlaendische station to check on the earlier, shuttle-service train for which I had not waited. The station master assured me he had noticed no one of President Benson's description get off that train. Back again I hurried to the Staats station to meet the later train from Paris, but again my search was fruitless.

Now I phoned the Hotel des Indes, where we were registered, and was told that President Benson had arrived. I figured that they must have been talking about my own arrival because they said that they expected him to return in a few minutes Somewhat confused and disappointed, I returned to the hotel.

As I entered my room at the hotel, there sat President Benson with Chaplain Badger.

"Why didn't you meet us at the station?" President Benson asked.

"How in the world did you get here?" I blurted out.

"We arrived on the train about which I wired you," he replied.

Then I explained that the station master had assured me that no passengers from Paris could possibly arrive on that train.

"Yes, I know," he said. "They told me that in Paris!"

I was flabbergasted, though I ought not to have been. After all, I had seen Brother Benson's faith and inspiration in action before—like the time when we made the emergency landing at North Platte, Nebraska, on the flight to New York. A blizzard grounded all planes there for two or three days, a delay unacceptable to our schedule. In a North Platte hotel room, Brother Benson suggested that we seek the Lord's guidance. Together we knelt in prayer at the bedside. There I learned something about Elder Benson's sweet but powerful humility.

Several long-distance phone calls by Elder Benson got us two reservations on an allegedly full train from North Platte to Chicago plus two seats on the first plane out of that city—despite the overburdened passenger lists caused by the snow blanketing the area. At Chicago, where there had been a three-day halt to air traffic, the sky cleared briefly and we boarded the only plane which left that day. As we took off, the blizzard resumed its fury.

The storm delayed our flight out of New York for one day, which gave us time to secure the remaining visas we needed. Two of the four engines were sputtering before we reached Gander, Newfoundland, and the problem was not entirely resolved by the ground maintenance crew curing our two-hour stop there; before we reached Ireland we were flying on three engines.

When my call first came, I knelt down with my wife June to ask the Lord for guidance and strength. As we prayed, one scripture repeated itself over and over in my mind: "And they shall go forth and none shall stay them, for I the Lord have commanded them" (D&C 1:5).

"None shall stay them!" I had had much occasion since then to reflect on those words. The remarkable way in which my exit from army life had been smoothed and expedited and the necessary passports and permits obtained—this was only the beginning. Being able to arrange with the American embassy for travel priorities reserved almost exclusively for top-flight military officers was another example. When I had gone to the London office of the European Air Transport Service of the army to get President Benson's plane ticket for the Paris flight, the official was sure there was some mistake He phoned the embassy to confirm that the priority certificate was in order. Even after receiving the confirmation, he continued to shake his head and mutter, "I can't believe it."

Yet with all this as background I still couldn't imagine how Elder Benson could have gotten from Paris to the correct hotel in The Hague—especially when I was watching all the trains. Piece by piece he told me his story.

"When we checked with the railway officials in Paris," he began, "it became evident that I had wired you incorrect information regarding our planned arrival. I was advised that we must plan to arrive a day later because the only connections with Holland necessitated entering that land from the eastern borders. The schedule I had given you pertained only to the local Dutch shuttle-service.

"We were almost resigned to taking the service they recommended," he continued. "It was then that I noticed a train on one of the tracks preparing to leave. 'Where is that train headed?' I asked the station master. 'Antwerp, Belgium,' he answered. I told him we would take that train and he assured me that we would lose an extra day because all connections between Antwerp and Holland had been cut off as a result of the war.

"But I felt impressed to board that train in spite of his protestations " Then President Benson described the poor condition of the train It consisted of broken-down cars with uncomfortable wooden-slatted seats, and sections of cardboard where once there had been window panes. All of these factors contributed to a rather unpleasant trip.

"When we arrived at Antwerp," he continued, "the station master was very upset and advised us that we would have to back-track somewhat and lose an extra day. Again I saw another train getting ready to leave and inquired where it was going. We were advised that this was a local shuttleservice which stopped at the Dutch border where the large bridge across the Maas river still lay in ruins. I felt impressed that we should board that train in spite of the station master's protests.

"When we reached the Maas river, we all had to pile out. As we stood picking up our luggage, we noticed an American army truck approaching us. Brother Badger flagged it down and, upon learning that there was a pontoon bridge nearby, he persuaded them to take us into Holland. When we arrived at the first little village on the Dutch side, we were pleasantly surprised to find this local shuttle-service waiting to take us into The Hague."

This was indeed an amazing series of events. I asked how they had been able to locate the hotel at which we were registered, since there were dozens of large hotels in the city.

President Benson said simply: "When Brother Badger and I got off the train and didn't find you waiting for us, we began walking in this direction. When I spotted this hotel, we came in to inquire about reservations and learned that this was the right hotel."

When President Benson inquired about our reservations for the flight to Denmark, I had to regretfully tell him what I had learned—no plane reservations and no other form of transportation. He replied "But we must leave tomorrow.... "Let me pray about it."

Before retiring, I had an opportunity to become fairly well acquainted with Chaplain Badger, who had received permission to accompany us on our tour of all the missions of Europe. He was very pleasant and extremely anxious to be of assistance. One of his large army duffel bags was bursting at the seams with foodstuffs sent by the LDS servicemen in Paris for the Dutch saints. We were to have the privilege of turning these supplies over to the acting mission presidency the following day. Their gratitude for these unexpected items was overwhelming.

Early the next morning President Benson called out, "Let's get busy!"

In view of his experience in getting to The Hague from Paris, I was prepared for just about anything. We went together to the Dutch Military Airlines, which had the only planes going to Copenhagen, and President Benson stressed to the officials the urgency of our mission. The official in charge replied, in substance: "Mr. Benson, we'd like to accommodate you. We've already discussed this matter with your secretary and you just can't get passage for about ten days. That's just the way things are. You Americans seem to forget that we've had a terrible war over here, but you'll just have to learn to put up with things as they are!"

President Benson was noticeably disappointed at this report. I felt that I was somewhat vindicated for my earlier efforts, that I had done all that could be done.

Now President Benson pursued another angle. We went to

the American Embassy, where our credentials enabled us to get an immediate audience with the ambassador. President Benson told him that the plane for Copenhagen was leaving shortly after noon today "We must be on that plane," he said, "and I'd appreciate it if you could arrange for our passage."

After learning of our efforts to date, the ambassador called the Dutch officials. At first they were adamant, but they finally agreed to restore to us the two spaces we had arranged for earlier. They assured him, however, that under no circumstances could they provide the third space which we needed for Brother Badger.

Undaunted by this development, President Benson accepted the ambassador's invitation to use his personal car and chauffeur, since the airport was about twenty-five miles distant and the departure time was very close.

When we arrived at Schiphol airport, we were met by the Dutch officials we had contacted earlier. They noticed that Chaplain Badger was with us and quickly emphasized that it was impossible to accommodate all three of us. President Benson assured them that he wasn't in the least discouraged. Then they showed us their passenger list. It was completely filled and they were preparing to load their passengers. But President Benson continued to feel an assurance that somehow Brother Badger would accompany us.

For some reason the plane was delayed for a few minutes. During this brief pause the airline officials noticed us still waiting there.

"How is it that you are still here?" they asked.

"Because all three of us just must get to Copenhagen today," replied President Benson.

"But we made it perfectly clear to you that this is impossible.

At this remark President Benson smiled and said firmly, "But we must!"

A strange look seemed to come over the official in charge as he said, "Well, then, you had better hurry!" We hurried out to the waiting plane and climbed into the bucket seats!

As we were boarding the plane, Brother Badger remarked: "President Benson, you have more influence, more power and authority with government officials, than any general in the

United States Army!" I certainly felt to concur with this remark. With each passing day the evidence continued to mount and assure us that the Lord was truly with this dedicated servant and his watchcare was over us daily.

It was an excellent flight lasting two hours and forty minutes, and we came in for a perfect landing.

When the airport limousine dropped us off at the city square, I suggested that we board the number 8 streetcar to go out to the mission home. Although I insisted that I knew what I was doing, Elder Benson must have doubted my memory; he had us take a taxicab in order not to get lost, particularly since it was growing dark. Using what little Danish I had learned before the war, I gave the driver the address of our destination and wrote it down for him. He had never heard of such a street. I suggested that he start driving and let me direct him to the mission home, which I did successfully, much to the amazement of all concerned. (After this experience, President Benson was willing to trust my judgment in such matters.)

At the mission home we were treated like long-lost brothers returned. They were so overjoyed and grateful. It seemed that nothing within their power was too good for us. President Orson B. West, the acting mission president, invited the branch presidency to come over to meet us. They showed us attractively printed handbills announcing that an apostle was to speak to the public on Sunday afternoon. They had also arranged for several newsmen to interview President Benson in the morning, this to be followed later in the day by a radio broadcast-interview over the Scandinavian radio network.

That evening we were served a delicious smorgasbord with all the butter and milk we could wish. By contrast with Britain and Holland, which were still on rationing, this was a land over-flowing with milk and honey.

Denmark in fact seemed to be better fixed for food than any other country in Europe. Even during the war years, we were told, they had plenty to eat and drink because of the cleverness with which the king had managed to rule his people in spite of the German occupation—a master stroke of diplomacy. (Clothing, on the other hand, was still in short supply.)

This may not be the whole story, however. When in August 1939 it seemed that war was inevitable, the First Presidency gave word that all missionaries in Germany were to be transferred to "neutral" countries. President Joseph Fielding Smith, who was then touring the European Missions, directed that missionaries from the East German Mission go to Denmark and those from the West German Mission go to Holland. Because Holland refused to permit the missionaries to enter, the missionaries from both German missions were sent to Denmark, where they were allowed to enter. Shortly after this, President Joseph Fielding Smith prophesied that "because the Danish people had helped the missionaries they would be blessed."[1]

While in Copenhagen, we visited the "Fruh Kirke" (The Church of Our Lady). Here were located the exquisite statues of Christ and the Twelve Apostles fashioned by Denmark's most famous sculptor, Bertel Thorvaldsen, who completed these beautiful works of art in 1838.

All the statues are sculptured from beautiful white Carrara Italian marble. Along the walls of the chief aisle are the big marble statues of the Twelve Apostles (Paul replacing Judas Iscariot). Over the high altar, surrounded by four large bronze candelabra, in a fine niche, is the famous statue of Christ, popularly known as the Christus. (A beautiful replica of this statue now graces the Bureau of Information exhibit hall in Temple Square, Salt Lake City.) Beneath the statue, chiseled in the marble, are the words of the Savior, "Come unto me." And hung above the statue are the stirring words, "This is my Son, the beloved one."

In this statue, Christ looks robust and strong, yet radiates a look of compassion which makes one almost expect the statue to speak. The work on all the statues is exquisite, but the Christus is without question Thorvaldsen's crowning masterpiece. Even the fingernails and the toenails are delicately sculptured. On each

[1]See Joseph F. McConkie, *True and Faithful The Life Story of Joseph Fielding Smith* (Salt Lake City: Bookcraft, 1971), p. 52.

genuine Thorvaldsen statue the small right toe is partially curled across the adjoining toe. This was his special trademark.

An attractive placard by the Christus, printed in several languages, read: "If you would behold the master's art, then bend your knees and look up." As one kneels, a beautiful transformation seems to take place. The statue fairly seems to breathe. One can see the veins and muscles. Tears seem to glisten in the Savior's eyes.

The marble Christus has all the appearance of life and vitality. Seeing the incomparable work of art was a profoundly moving experience.

The radio interview with President Benson later that afternoon was broadcast live by means of a portable broadcasting unit and was also recorded for rebroadcast on the entire Scandinavian radio network that evening. The person conducting the interview made a brief announcement at its conclusion, inviting the people of Denmark to attend the special meeting the following day so that they might see and hear a real live apostle! Earlier in the day Elder Benson had been interviewed by four leading newspapers, all of which published favorable and friendly accounts of the interviews.

Five hundred and seventy-five persons attended the announced public meeting the following afternoon—the largest group since the Copenhagen chapel had been dedicated in 1931. Every available seat was taken, and those standing were crowded to the limit. President Benson delivered a stirring discourse on the three questions: Where did I come from? Why am I here? Where will I go from here?

On Monday morning Brother Gregersen, the branch president, came over to the mission home for a short visit. President Benson, in a jovial mood, tried to catch him off guard by saying: "For years I have heard that 'there's something rotten in Denmark' and I just wondered if you could tell me what it is?"

Apparently assuming the name Benson to be of Swedish origin (because of its "son" ending), the branch president countered quickly, "The only thing rotten in Denmark is the Swedes that live here!" And so began another day….

Later that afternoon President Benson and Brother Badger returned to the mission home in a fancy German Horch car, which had been custom-built for one of the German generals who had been in Denmark during the military occupation. It had a straight sixteen-cylinder engine with six speeds forward. The Danish driver assigned as our chauffeur seemed to delight in "winding her up." When he reached one of the super-highways—practically deserted since the war—he just had to demonstrate what the car would do. The next thing we knew he was in sixth gear speeding along at 235 kilometers—about 145 m.p.h. I had never gone so fast on land in my life before. I was seated in the back seat of this club-coupe-type body with Brother Badger and was delighted to see President Benson in the front seat holding his hat tightly on his head with the aid of both hands!

It was difficult to say "goodbye" to the Danish saints who assembled at the station to see us off for Sweden.

The water system on the train was frozen, and this resulted in a complete lack of both water and heat. The ground was heavily covered with a blanket of snow and the weather was near zero These factors made our sleeping a bit uncomfortable in spite of heavy blankets.

Waiting to greet us at the Stockholm railway station were Mission President Eben R. T. Blomquist, newly arrived from the United States and the local branch president, Brother Einar Johannson. That evening we attended a special public service attended by 225 members and their friends. Local concert artists furnished lovely instrumental music and an excellent choir rendered beautiful singing.

President Benson's remarks carried a strong spirit of conviction to those in the audience. They were visibly moved by the overflowing spirit of love that was present and were reluctant to see the evening draw to a close. In beginning his remarks, President Benson had said: "I wish so much that I might speak to you in your own language, but I feel sure that we shall understand one another, because there is a language more powerful than the language of any nation: it is the language of the gospel of love." It was evident that he had used that language to the full understanding of his audience.

In his address, Elder Benson felt impressed to relate some of the events surrounding the selection of President George Albert Smith as the Prophet, Seer, and Revelator after the passing of President Heber J. Grant. Among other things he said:

"I have never felt the Spirit of the Lord stronger than when President George Albert Smith was set apart in the temple.... Various rumors from enemies of the Church were being circulated that certain members of the Council of the Twelve were aspiring to be president.

"In our meeting together, President Grant's two counselors took their places in the Council of the Twelve according to their seniority. President David O. McKay sat next to President George F. Richards and President J. Reuben Clark, Jr., next to Elder Albert E. Bowen, being senior to him. President George Albert Smith, as President of the Council of the Twelve, was the presiding officer.

"As the meeting progressed, I have never felt so powerfully the Spirit of the Lord. There was no feeling of selfishness or vain ambition present. The Spirit dictated to every man present whom the Lord wanted and every man in that council was brought to tears. When the Spirit of the Lord is felt so powerfully that fourteen strong, mature men are all simultaneously brought to tears and the spirit of divine unity is manifest, as it was on that occasion, one cannot help but know that there is a Greater Power at the head of this Church than man.

"Before the meeting was ended, President George Albert Smith was sustained unanimously and ordained President of The Church of Jesus Christ of Latter-day Saints and as God's Prophet, Seer, and Revelator. President David O. McKay served as mouth for the quorum in ordaining him. Later, at the October General Conference of the Church, he was unanimously sustained by the body of the Church.

"At no time to this day have I heard a single word of opposition.... I testify that there is unity in the councils of the Church.... Action is never taken in the councils of the Church unless all are unanimous."

The Swedish saints had done an outstanding job during the war years. They had maintained nearly twenty full-time local missionaries in the field during the entire time. Their record of convert baptisms was higher annually than the years immediately preceding the war when there were many more missionaries in that land. Their total tithing had increased 300 percent and their fast offerings 600 percent over the prewar figures. In addition, they enjoyed an attendance of approximately 85 percent of the membership at their sacrament meetings.

We were signing autographs and shaking hands for nearly an hour and a half before leaving for our hotel.

Before President Benson and I left for this mission in Europe, we had been set apart and given special blessings by the First Presidency. In President Benson's blessing he was promised that through his efforts the gospel would be preached in lands where it had never been preached before. A prelude to the partial fulfillment of that promise took place the morning after our first meeting with the Swedish saints.

That morning we met with ten local full-time missionaries, members of the mission office staff, and two or three other local saints. Together we enjoyed a soul-enriching missionary testimony meeting in the upper part of the chapel. Although we Americans couldn't understand the Swedish language in which the testimonies were given, we could feel their strength and sincerity.

When President Benson arose, he was filled to overflowing with that same sweet spirit. Among other things he mentioned that throughout the previous day and far into the night he had felt impressed by the Spirit that the gospel should be taken to the people of Finland.

"As a servant of the Lord," he said, "I call upon you, Brother Fritz Johansson, to go to Finland as a missionary, to open the way for the preaching of the gospel among that wonderful people. You may take as a companion whomever you and President Blomquist may select. If you go humbly in the spirit of your calling, many of the honest in heart will be glad and willing to receive your testimony and be baptized into the Church."

What a glorious pronouncement! We were all moved to tears of gratitude. Brother Johansson beamed all over as he accepted this call and was set apart with a blessing and a promise. I was particularly impressed that after serving for nearly seven years as acting mission president during the war years, he gladly accepted another call to open Finland for the preaching of the gospel. None who were in attendance could ever forget that occasion or the spirit of inspiration which was there made manifest.

That evening we were dinner guests of Brother Einar Johannson, the branch president. He took us to one of Stockholm's most fashionable cafes, the "Gondola," which is suspended in the air by cables attached to the underside of the bridge-like walk leading to the city elevator which takes people to the lower part of the city. The mission home and our hotel were located on the high cliff overlooking the city.

We dined for nearly five hours. The plentiful food included a complete lavish smorgasbord plus ten main courses and a number of side dishes, desserts, etc. We sampled thirty kinds of cheese—everything from yak and reindeer cheese to goat and other dairy cheeses. Never had I eaten so much for so long a period of time and enjoyed it so thoroughly.

As we concluded this indescribable feast, President Benson commented to Brother Johannson that it appeared to him that the Swedish people live to eat rather than eat to live. This Brother Johannson readily admitted, saying, with a twinkle in his eye, "Ya, but we enjoy it!"

From our vantage point we could look out upon the beauty of this "Venice of the North," as it is affectionately known. Beautiful strains of classical and semi-classical music, provided by a violin-piano team, enhanced this perfect setting.

It was nearing midnight when we returned to the mission home. There we knelt with the missionaries to leave behind a blessing and to ask the Lord's watchcare over us in our further travels. Though the hour was late, the entire group walked with us to the railway station in the subzero weather, many of them wearing their heavy Swedish fur caps.

This walk gave us an excellent opportunity to see this lovely capital in its beautiful nighttime setting. On a high hill overlooking the city is the king's castle. The city is crisscrossed by several canals and picturesque bridges, the architecture varying from ancient to medieval and ultra-modern. Wrapped in a blaze of brilliant neon lights, in this respect the city resembles the most modern American cities. No wonder it is often called the Jewel of the North.

Imagine our surprise at being greeted at the station by another large contingent of saints. They formed a large semicircle and sang many happy songs, among them that old favorite "Farewell to Thee" sung in English! It was a heartwarming experience. As we pulled out of the station, the saints continued to wave their handkerchiefs until we were entirely out of sight.

We were on a Norwegian train which lacked heat and was visibly short of normal accommodations. This situation did not facilitate restful sleeping, but the memory of the day just ended seemed to compensate fully for any inconveniences we might have encountered from time to time.

The Norwegian customs officials, who aroused us before 6 a.m. to check our passports and baggage, continued checking on various matters until we arrived at Olso. While we didn't at first appreciate the early call, it did give us an opportunity to enjoy the magnificent scenery

The houses were widely scattered. Here and there we could see groups of hardy skiers. Everything was covered heavily with a blanket of ermine-white snow. I was fascinated by this scenic land of rugged mountains, dense forests, and jewel-like lakes.

Arriving in Oslo, we were greeted warmly by President A. Richard Peterson and his family. Accompanying them was Sherman A. Gowans, an LDS army officer attached to the American Embassy.

Most of the afternoon I spent in helping the retiring and the new mission secretaries prepare an audit of the mission records so that they could get started with the revised system of record keeping. These records were difficult to untangle, the financial figures having been juggled during the Nazi occupation. This was done to avoid the complete confiscation of properties by the occupying military powers.

An unusual incident in this connection was the report of Brother Olaf Sonsteby, acting mission president during the war. He was a tailor by trade. As the occupying powers began to take possession of all denominational funds, an interesting chase began. Brother Sonsteby placed the mission funds in one bank after another. When it became evident that he could no longer pursue this course with safety, he was forced to bury the funds in the ground. When he went to uncover these funds after the liberation of his country, he was faced with a unique problem.

"When I recovered these funds from the ground where I had buried them," he said, "I found there were 37,000 crowns more money than I had buried. And I don't know how to account for this extra amount!" Here was one case where the "buried talents" increased. His genuine concern was relieved when I suggested that we merely show the increase as miscellaneous donations received from an unknown source.

In the evening newspaper was a disquieting note. The police building in Tel Aviv had been rocked that day by an explosion as Palestine terrorists renewed their raids on police headquarters in both Tel Aviv and Haifa. President Benson assured us, however, that when the current disturbances ceased, the Jewish people would be found securely in their old homeland and would be blessed by the Lord in rebuilding it. It was reassuring to hear his reaction to such incidents. Events of the intervening years have borne out his words.

Our evening meeting with saints and friends was a spiritual feast. Beautiful music was furnished by a chorus of eighty voices accompanied by a well-balanced string orchestra. We learned that this Oslo choir is famous throughout Scandinavia, and even President Benson volunteered that it was the best choir he had ever heard except for the Salt Lake Tabernacle Choir!

To those assembled, President Benson made a significant promise. Said he:

> "I promise you as a servant of God that if you will live true to the covenants you have made with him and will live the gospel as it has been restored, every blessing you might receive by living close to the temples shall be granted unto you, even the celestial

kingdom of God.

"God judges us not only by what we do, but by what we would do and desire to do if we had the opportunity. He will not withhold any blessing from us of which we are truly worthy."

After this meeting Brother Gowans invited us to share the lovely accommodations of his home for the night. This home formerly belonged to a Norwegian millionaire who had been imprisoned after the war as a Nazi collaborator and war profiteer. The walls were covered with many rare and expensive oil paintings while the furniture and the oriental carpets added a note of luxury to which we were not accustomed.

Brother Badger and I were required to bunk together in a single bed—a bit uncomfortable, but welcome after the restless nights on the sleepers to and from Stockholm. President Benson slept in a large bed above which hung an exquisite, life-sized painting.

Although my acquaintanceship with President Benson thus far had been a brief one, I was beginning to realize what a blessed privilege was mine in working with him. Never had I met a man of God who was so humble, so grateful for loyalty and kindness rendered, so genuinely and deeply emotional and receptive to that which is good and pure, a man who has such an all-consuming love for the children of our Father. Since our arrival he had been able to do more in less time, and that more thoroughly and effectively, than I had ever dreamed to be possible.

We learned that until 1925 Oslo was known as Christiania, named in honor of King Christian of Denmark. He founded the present city in 1624 upon the ruins of the former city of Oslo, whose history goes back to 1047. National pride caused the Norwegians to restore the city's original name after all those years. The fiord on which the city is located is still known by many as Christiania Fiord.

The Folk Museum contains three famous ships which were used by the Norse Vikings. All of them were excavated in fairly modern times. As we gazed upon them, we marveled at the daring of those people in coming to America in such small vessels nearly a thousand years ago.

After our hasty but enjoyable "Cook's Tour," we boarded a C-47 army transport plane manned by a British crew. The temperature outside was 20° below zero, but as we reached the seven-thousand-foot level in flight it dropped sharply to 40° below. There was no heat in the plane, no insulation to cover the steel floor or the aluminum hull. Sitting in the canvas bucket seats, before we arrived in Copenhagen we were nearly frozen stiff. It was with extreme difficulty that we were able to deplane. And snow was still falling in spite of the subzero temperatures.

We attended an evening meeting in Copenhagen the following day. President Benson spoke of many things. He mentioned two case histories worthy of note

The first concerned a young LDS fellow en route by plane from Washington, D.C., to Canada to accept employment. Weather conditions necessitated making a landing on an emergency landing field in Western Pennsylvania. Passengers were told that they would be there for several hours. Through the trees they noticed a light. Upon investigating, they discovered it to be a CCC camp.[2]

The young men in the camp were just sitting down for supper and invited the passengers to join them. Hot coffee was being served, and although the LDS fellow was rather strict in his Church standards under ordinary conditions, since it was quite cold and he was where no one knew him he decided to drink some coffee.

As he began to drink it, the young man seated next to him asked him where he was from.

"Washington, D.C., but formerly Utah."

"Are you a Mormon by any chance?"

"Yes, I am."

Upon receiving this answer, the young CCC man said, "But not a very good one, are you!"

---

[2]Civilian Conservation Corps. This was an employment relief program instituted by President Franklin D. Roosevelt which operated from 1933 through 1942.

He then proceeded to explain that he had lived for some time at a CCC camp near St. George, Utah, where he had come to appreciate that good Mormons observe Church standards strictly. It developed that he had attended several Church services while there and was quite familiar with the Word of Wisdom.

President Benson's second account concerned a certain bishop who frequently ate at a nearby Chinese cafe. Following a session of stake conference he was met there by another local bishop who also frequented this place. When their order was taken, both men ordered milk.

As the Chinese waiter placed their orders before them, he asked rather curiously: "How is it that when you gentlemen come here alone you always order coffee with your meals, but when you come together you always order milk?"

Through these excellent illustrations President Benson stressed the importance of recognizing that the eyes of the world are upon the people of this Church. He concluded by pleading with the saints to continue to be "a peculiar people observing strictly the will of God."

When we left Copenhagen, all three of us were warmly dressed for our flight back to London. But the British military plane was an unheated freight plane like the one we had taken from Oslo a few days earlier. At seven thousand feet altitude it was so intensely cold that we had to resort to moving around in the plane to keep our blood circulating. Finally we were so thoroughly chilled that we were unable to move without extreme effort. The wings of our plane kept icing up, causing some of the few passengers on board with us to become very uneasy. But I, for one, never worried when I was traveling with President Benson on the Lord's business. I relied upon the blessing given me by President J. Reuben Clark, Jr., when he had set me apart:

"...You are going back—and under the blessings of the Lord you will return—among the people with whom you formerly labored on your first mission.

"...We seal these blessings upon you together with health and strength, that you may go in peace and return in safety, all through your faith and faithfulness..."

When we finally landed at Croydon airport just outside London about four hours later, we were a sad-looking lot. At each step our knees would buckle under us. Each foot felt like a large block of ice and there was virtually no feeling in our legs. Never had I experienced such difficulty in walking.

By bathing our legs in cold water upon reaching our mission headquarters, we were gradually able to restore some feeling in our limbs. Through the blessings of the Lord we were spared the complications accompanying severe frostbite. Our gratitude that night was overwhelming.

Mail was stacked in huge piles upon President Benson's desk. He continued dictating steadily from the moment we arrived until late that evening. Since our larder was empty, I had to purchase such meager food supplies as were available to us on our ration coupons before beginning the seemingly endless typing of letters.

During our absence no heat had been channeled to our rooms, so every room was thoroughly chilled. Thanks to the several electric fireplaces in the home we were gradually able to lessen the cold dampness, although in so doing we were using far more electricity for a longer period of time than governmental regulations permitted.

We felt very blessed to have this accommodation. Bomb damage had made office and living space very scarce, and when we first arrived in London, British Mission President Hugh B. Brown had suggested that we use facilities at the mission office for the time being. Feeling that we needed more central accommodation, President Benson declined this generous offer, and we set out house-hunting.

We became acutely aware of the seriousness of the housing shortage as we began our search. No major reconstruction work had been undertaken in the entire city since the war. Bombed shops and houses still stretched their smoke-blackened, naked, partially-standing walls to the leaden sky. Some sections of London had escaped miraculously, but others were heavily hit, especially during the waning months of the war when Germany started using its V-1 and V-2 rockets. Even so, the destruction on parts of the Continent was overwhelming by comparison.

Our search finally took us to one of London's most fashionable sections the area of Bond and Brook Streets. We walked into an old dismal-looking courtyard through a narrow alley. From the exterior, the place we examined looked very plain and uninteresting, but the interior of the apartment exceeded our fondest expectations. Both of us felt that it was the Lord's answer to our fervent prayers. The following morning we moved into our new headquarters.

It turned out that we had rented a section of the former home of the noted musician, George Frederick Handel, where he had composed his great masterpiece "the Messiah." In appearance it resembled somewhat a medieval castle. Our section gave us three rooms and a bath, together with kitchen privileges. Entering the apartment through a long hallway was reminiscent of entering a large museum. The door to the living room had a heavy wrought-iron latch like that on the door of an old castle. The walls were all tastefully paneled with large walnut squares. Later we discovered that there were many hidden storage areas and concealed passageways behind these panels leading to other rooms in other parts of this sizeable home.

All the windows had heavy wrought-iron gratings, giving virtually the security of a prison. The window drapes were made of very heavy, luxurious velvet. The home was tastefully furnished, having a beautiful grand piano and oriental carpets in the living room.

Here we had set up our home and our office. With a typewriter, plus discarded dictaphone equipment I had salvaged from the damp attic of the British Mission office and then laboriously rejuvenated, we were ready to go.

The equipment certainly got a good workout after our return from the initial tour of Europe. Brother Badger stayed with us, bedding down on a couch in the front room. He retired early, while I continued typing away until the wee hours of the morning. It took several long days work to complete the correspondence. Yet in spite of long hours, little sleep, cold and damp weather, and generally inadequate meals, the Lord continued to bless and sustain me. I was able to avoid colds and carry on my necessary mission activities with a minimum of difficulty.

As I looked back at this first month in Europe, it seemed almost unbelievable that so much had happened. The Lord certainly had showered his blessings upon us!

In a special report to the First Presidency, which we included as a part of the official European Mission History, President Benson summarized our recent trip as follows:

> The general condition of the Saints is improving daily. Spiritually it has been good throughout the war and was perhaps never better than it is now. Mission leaders everywhere report that in their experience the Saints have never so completely lived the law of tithing and kept the Word of Wisdom and otherwise maintained the standards of the Church. While the Saints have been called upon to endure hardships almost beyond description, in many cases, yet they have remained hopeful and optimistic, even during occupation of their countries by a foreign enemy when at times they feared for their very lives.

> During the past two or three weeks we have ridden in unheated trains, trucks, and airplanes in order to visit the various missions, but in every instance we were greeted upon arrival with such love and warmth of spirit that any hardships encountered in our travels were soon forgotten. Probably the gospel has never been so fully appreciated by the Saints in Europe as during the recent war period. Already we have come to love them deeply and I am sure we cannot say enough in praise of their devotion to the truth and their love of the General Authorities of the Church.

chapter two

"I Shall Go Before Them"

Paris had just had its heaviest snowfall since 1867. At Orly Field, the airport for Paris at which we were scheduled to land, the landing strips were rendered unuseable by several feet of snow. We had to seek other means of entering France.

The most convenient train departed from London's Waterloo Station at 10:00 p.m. When we reached the Channel, we boarded the steamer bound for Dieppe, France. According to our tickets, we had first-class sleepers. When we boarded the steamer, we were required to stand in a long line to be assigned to our cabins. Imagine our surprise when we were sent down to a former drawing room which contained about forty double-decker bunk beds, each with one blanket and no sheets! (Incidentally the trip by train and steamer cost half again as much as the same trip by plane.)

Apparently we had been given the last two available bunks, poor as they were, because the people behind us were only given space on seats. When these had been assigned, the remaining passengers had to stand, even though they had all been charged first-class fares. (This was a foretaste of conditions we would repeatedly experience as a result of the disorganization resulting from war.)

Fortunately, Chaplain Badger came to the rescue. He was able to get us transferred to a broken-down stateroom for an extra $2.00 per person. These accommodations, though very poor by American standards, gave us a little more privacy and we were able to get some much-needed rest.

When we pulled into Dieppe harbor, just as the dawn was breaking, we were greeted by the worst scene of destruction we had witnessed to that time. Most of the buildings were nothing but a twisted mass of battered ruins. All bridges had been blasted and remained crumpled, useless heaps. The harbor itself was a sickening scene of desolation and debris. This was the Dieppe which took such a terrific beating on D-Day, not the picturesque Dieppe of earlier days.

This scene was repeated in village after village along the way to Paris, but we were informed that such devastation was mild compared with that which would greet us upon our arrival in Germany. Nevertheless, it was an appalling sight.

We were provided with accommodations at the Terrasse Hotel by two of our fine servicemen, Captains Sherman L. Brinton and Thomas L. Adams. They made room for us in their own quarters. Both these exceptional Latter-day Saints had accomplished wonders with LDS servicemen in the area.

In Paris, President Benson called on the colonel in charge of communications with Germany. He explained to him that we wished to make arrangements to visit our saints in Germany so we could organize our forces for receiving and distributing our relief and rehabilitation supplies and get our people organized to begin the mammoth job of spiritual rejuvenation. He then reviewed with him our projected itinerary for traveling through all the four military zones in Germany and Austria as well as making a trip into Czechoslovakia.

When the colonel saw the itinerary he fairly blurted out: "Mr. Benson, are you crazy? Don't you realize there has been a war here and that to date no civilian travelers have been permitted to enter these military areas to conduct the kind of work you suggest? At the present time we have no provisions for taking care of visitors. All fond, accommodations and travel facilities are restricted for use by the military."

President Benson quietly asked whether or not permission might be granted if we could purchase a car to make the trip. The colonel answered that cars were nearly impossible to purchase in America, let alone in Europe where there was an acute shortage He advised us further that no gasoline was being made available to civilians in Germany, so that method of travel was out of the question.

After the colonel had made several other incredulous outbursts, President Benson asked: "If I could arrange for transportation, food, and military permission, do you think we might make it?"

With a look of amazement the colonel replied: "If all those things could be arranged, you might get into the American Zone, but to arrange for these things is impossible!"

This did not dismay President Benson As we left he turned to us and said, "Let's get busy!"

Before the day ended we had purchased one reasonably serviceable Dodge army truck from the Army Liquidation Commission and had contacted several important French governmental and manufacturing officials to determine the feasibility of purchasing some new French cars. More visits would have to be made, but President Benson was optimistic and had courage born of faith.

The following day President Benson decided that Brother Badger and I should drive the Army truck to Holland for use of the Dutch Mission in the distribution of their welfare supplies. We left at about 3:00 p.m. for Liege, Belgium. It turned out to be quite a trip.

The roads were poor in many places and much of the time they were slippery with ice and snow. Along the way we had a good view of the French landscape with its bombed-out villages, blown-up bridges, etc. In fact, we did not cross a single bridge that was an original prewar model. Along both sides of the road were mountainous supplies of ammunition stretching out mile after mile. Here and there we could see many destroyed American tanks and some German tanks and planes as well. Shell holes dotted the landscape in every direction. All in all it presented a sobering picture of the uselessness and wastefulness of war.

At about 8:30 p.m. we crossed the border into Belgium. Since we were in an American Army truck, the border officials didn't even stop us, so my passport and visa were not checked or stamped.

About thirty miles south of Liege we encountered a very dense fog that made driving slow and hazardous. We were barely crawling along when a young girl flagged us down and asked if we could take her aunt and her grandmother with us into Liege. They had missed the last available bus. Realizing their predicament, we decided to be helpful.

Since the back of the truck was loaded with gasoline, oil, and luggage, we had to make room for them in the front seat. The auntie was in her late thirties, while the grandmother was a spry woman of about seventy. Although they could speak no English, we managed to carry on an intelligible conversation.

I had to hold the grandmother on my lap for the first fifteen miles, at which time I took over the job of driving and let Brother Badger furnish the seating facilities for the grandmother. Both of us were glad when we finally reached the outskirts of Liege and discharged the passengers. The grandmother had loaded in quite a few fresh eggs, a number of which were broken by the time we arrived, but she managed to pick out a half-dozen and a few tomatoes to reward us for our courtesy.

Brother Badger had spent some time in Liege with the Devignez family at the close of the war, so we were able to find their home without too much difficulty. It was well past midnight when we awakened the family to inquire about a place to sleep. Both of us were tired, dirty with grease, etc., from the army truck. In spite of our sad appearance, we were warmly welcomed and provided with comfortable beds for the night.

Paul Devignez was acting mission president in Belgium during the war years and rendered outstanding service. His brother, also a faithful member, was killed in the closing days of the war after having been miraculously spared many times during several crucial battles. We lost a total of seven or eight Belgian members as a result of war casualties.

Dawn was rapidly approaching but Sister Devignez insisted on preparing a meal for us before we retired. Having driven all the way without stopping to eat, we were pleased to accept her invitation. Those beds felt extremely comfortable after the rough truck ride.

Our Church building in Liege had not been seriously damaged even though Liege was considered to be one of the worst-bombed cities in Belgium. All nine bridges in the city had been demolished.

The morning after our arrival we visited mile after mile of ruins on both sides of the river. Much of the heavy fighting of the Battle of the Bulge had taken place in this general area. Construction work was already in evidence.

Through welfare packages which had been sent to our saints, our membership was faring better than many. They were facing the future with confidence and seemed to be in an excellent spiritual condition On the whole, the situation in Belgium had much improved since the close of war. Many items of food were available in small quantities, as were items of clothing, but the prices were too high for the average family.

In Antwerp I located a number of storage and warehouse facilities which we felt might be suitable for storing some of our welfare supplies for later distribution. President Benson suggested before we left on this trip that Antwerp might become one of our major receiving centers. We also investigated the possibility of handling forwarding activities out of Antwerp through the International Red Cross and were assured that that organization would be happy to furnish such assistance.

At the Dutch border we met President Cornelius Zappey of that mission. He was almost beside himself with joy as we turned over the truck to him and showed him the ample supply of gasoline which would help him get his job of welfare distribution under way. We wished him Godspeed, and he began his journey back to The Hague. Since the Army truck still had its army insignias and license plates, he encountered no difficulty in getting home. This truck proved to be a real boon in getting welfare supplies distributed throughout Holland.

Arriving in Brussels, we learned that there were no sleepers available for us on the train to Paris. The train was divided into two sections—one for military personnel and the other for civilians. After some fancy talking, Brother Badger, as a chaplain, was able to get a single lower berth for himself in the military section.

That took care of him, but I was still faced with a problem.

To all appearances, I had entered Belgium illegally, since my passport and visa had not been stamped when I entered the country. The customs officials would certainly be suspicious about me. Brother Badger and I both felt that it would be dangerous to have my passport checked—which would happen if I were to ride on the civilian portion of the train. Yet I was not permitted on the military section.

Being an ingenious person, Brother Badger lent me his army raincoat and had me board the military section loaded down with his baggage while he carted mine. Together we entered his sleeping compartment. He explained our difficult circumstances to his traveling companion, and together they hid me in the space under the seat until after the customs officials had made their necessary inspection. I was nearly suffocating but hardly dared breathe for fear of being discovered. Once our door was locked, I was permitted to come out of hiding.

Using our clothing and the ladder provided to reach the upper berth, we made a rude mattress for me and I was able to sleep through the night in comparative safety and comfort.

We arrived in Paris at about six o'clock the next morning. By taking several precautions I was able to get off the military section of the train without arousing undue suspicion.

President Benson was pleased with our reports about our transfer of the truck and the storage facilities and services in Antwerp. In our absence he had been able to arrange for the purchase of two new French Citroen cars, a feat which had necessitated his visiting thirty French governmental officials and industrial executives. These were two of the first cars off the French production line after the war. We used one for our travels and left the other one in Paris for President James L. Barker of the French Mission.

Both these cars were small four-door sedans, similar to the 1932 model Fords. They had a step-down design which made the occupants ride low to the surface of the road. They were considered economical; and while neither as comfortable nor as roomy as the smallest American car, they provided much-needed transportation. All of us were thrilled that the Lord had heard our prayers and answered them in this manner.

Having necessary transportation, and having made arrangements with the French government for a limited supply of gasoline—sufficient to take us to the Swiss border—we approached a rather surprised colonel. There was something about President Benson's humble, confident manner that struck a responsive chord this time, and within a few minutes the necessary military orders had been prepared for us to enter the American Zone of Germany and pass through the French Zone en route.

While the colonel seriously doubted our ability to secure additional permission from General McNarney in Frankfurt, who was in charge of all American forces in Europe, he agreed to these special orders for the first two strictly American civilians to enter these areas.

What a glorious demonstration of the power of the Lord! A few days previously, all of these developments were considered to be impossibilities, humanly speaking. Today they had become realities. The three of us were highly elated and most grateful as we recognized the hand of God in these accomplishments. They signified to us that the Lord was anxious for us to move ahead with all possible haste in accomplishing the tremendous job of physical and spiritual rehabilitation of our saints in Europe.

Since Paris had been respected as an "open city" during the war, it suffered no appreciable damage, but as we entered the outlying sections, we passed through village after village which showed sickening evidence of the ravages of war. In many sections the highways were in a deplorable condition caused not only by the heavy military traffic during the war and since, but also by the severe weather of the winter just ending.

As we traveled toward Switzerland, we spent many pleasant hours in conversation and in singing together. Brother Badger sang bass, President Benson sang the melody, and I provided suitable harmony. President Benson did most of the driving.

Our trip took us sixteen hours. How good it was to arrive safely at the lovely mission home in Basel, Switzerland, and to be greeted warmly there by Brother and Sister Max Zimmer!

chapter three

"Be Not Dismayed"

Max Zimmer, acting Swiss Mission President, accompanied us the following morning to attend a district conference being held in Karlsruhe, Germany.

The destruction at Dieppe and Liege did not begin to compare in fury with the desolation that greeted us in city after city in Germany. Most of the streets had been cleared of primary rubble, but in every direction was mute evidence of the destructiveness and effectiveness of Allied bombing and shelling.

The city of Freiburg in the French zone of Germany presented a sickening sight of stunned, listless people shuffling among the blackened, twisted ruins of this once-beautiful city. It was in an almost complete state of ruin. The nearby city of Pforzheim was considered to be 90 percent destroyed. When we arrived at Karlsruhe we were horrified by the wanton destruction that greeted us. Such scenes cannot be adequately described. They must be witnessed and experienced to be understood and comprehended. But they all bear witness that war is hell!

Along the way we passed groups of older people and children going to church. Many were in rags and barefooted. At the approach of our car they became frightened—almost to the point of hysteria in some cases—and many ran for the nearest shelter to hide from us. When we blew our horn, it was easy to see the fear and anxiety etched upon their faces. Yet they seemed at times to be so completely unnerved that they just stood transfixed in the roadway, apparently unable to summon the will and the energy to make it to the edge of the road.

Fortunately, the farming communities had largely been spared. Here everything looked orderly and beautifully green. People seemed to breathe more freely and walk more briskly. All along the way, however, were multiplied scenes of railroad bombings. Wherever a large industrial building had been standing, nothing remained but a mass of wreckage.

Upon arriving at Karlsruhe, we made inquiries to learn where our saints might be meeting in district conference. Finally, there was pointed out to us a sizeable area of almost completely demolished buildings and we were told that they were probably meeting somewhere in that section.

Parking our car near massive heaps of twisted steel and concrete, we climbed over several large piles of rubble and threaded our way between the naked blasted walls in the general direction which had been pointed out to us. As we viewed the desolation on all sides of us, our task seemed hopeless. Then we heard the distant strains of "Come, Come Ye Saints" being sung in German. We were overjoyed. No strains of music were ever more welcome!

We hurried in the direction of the sound of the singing and arrived at a badly scarred building which still had several usable rooms. In one of the rooms we found 260 joyous saints still in conference, although it was already long past their dismissal time. (They had already been in session over three hours that afternoon, but had been hoping and praying that we might arrive in time to meet with them.)

As we entered the room, the closing strains of this beloved Mormon hymn swelled to a crescendo of joyousness that overwhelmed us. Sister Betty Baier Dahl and her sister, both formerly from Nuremberg, recognized me and cried out excitedly, "Brother Babbel! Brother Babbel."

With tears of gratitude streaming down our cheeks, we went as quickly as possible to the improvised stand. Never have I seen President Benson so deeply and visibly moved as on that occasion. For me, especially, it was heart-warming to be back in the midst of loyal friends. The entire audience rose to its feet to pay silent tribute to President Benson and to get a better look at us as we moved to the front.

This blasted former schoolroom was poorly lighted and ventilated. There was no heat and it was a chilly day. Seating accommodations were very poor and many of those present were visibly shivering from the cold. Several were dressed in shredded rags. The price of pain, tension and lingering starvation was clearly etched on many faces, but there was nevertheless a reverent air of expectancy and breathless excitement. The building was crowded beyond its capacity, but the audience was hushed in silence and anxiously waiting to hear from this choice servant of the Lord. In those few moments before President Benson arose to speak, it was a great joy to see on the stand and in the congregation dozens of familiar faces, grown haggard in many cases but now wreathed in rapturous smiles In a moment, President Benson arose and said:

"My heart is filled with gratitude, my brothers and sisters, as I look into your upturned faces. My heart goes out to you in the pure love of God.

"While I am grateful for this opportunity, I came here with a heavy heart. As we rode through your green and fruitful land, I saw in every town and hamlet the frightful result of man's disobedience to the laws of God.

"I support none nor condemn any for what has happened. God will be the judge and his judgments will be just because he sees not only the results of our decisions, but judges us by the intent of our hearts as well.

"The fruits of disobedience are everywhere in evidence. As I witnessed for the first time the appalling desolation and the almost unbelievable destruction that has taken place, I could not help but project myself and my family into your midst. As I began to contemplate what unspeakable hardships we would have had to endure had we lived in your land these past several years, I began to appreciate what a frightening and heart-sickening experience must have been yours. Then it dawned upon me just how priceless is our heritage of the restored gospel of Jesus Christ which is, after all, not only the most precious boon we enjoy, but the only really worthwhile enduring aspect of this life.

"As I look into your tear-stained eyes and see many of you virtually in rags and at death's door, yet with a smile upon your cracked lips and the light of love and understanding shining in your eyes, I know that you have been true to your covenants, that you have been clean, that you have not permitted hatred and bitterness to fill your hearts. You—many of you—are some of the Lord's choicest witnesses of the fruits of the gospel of Jesus Christ.

"No nation can escape the horrors of war unless its people live in accordance with God's word.... We always have been and will continue to be against war. Christ said no man should rule unjustly over his brethren. A violation of this profound truth will always sow the seeds of war and destruction.... Yet we have also been admonished to be loyal to those who have power over us. And almost without exception you have been loyal to your country even while abhorring those principles manifest in your government which were completely out of harmony with the gospel of Jesus Christ.

"We have known something of your terrible hardships. Our hearts have gone out to you in the pure love of God, which is stronger than death. We love you! We are grateful for your devotion, for your faith and your loyalty to the cause of the Master.... We have received sufficient records to know that you have done a wonderful work.

"There is a language in the gospel of Jesus Christ that can be understood even though we do not speak the same language. I feel that same spirit here today.

"We hope to be able to extend real relief to the suffering among you within the next few days, particularly those who find themselves as homeless refugees. We are here with the approval of the President of the United States. Our own governmental, military and State Department officials have been extending the finest kind of cooperation and we are very much encouraged that with God's help we shall be able to carry out his divine purposes concerning you and your temporal as well as your eternal welfare.

"We are all brothers and sisters. We are all members of the Church of Jesus Christ—the kingdom of God on earth. We accept wholeheartedly the statement of the Master that 'We are our brother's keeper.'

"If we are permitted to carry on our program as it has been designed under the inspiration of the Almighty, we shall be able to bring you real physical and spiritual help. It is not a plan that man has worked out; it is the Lord's plan. It is the only plan that will work. Of this fact I bear humble testimony as one of the Lord's special witnesses.

"Any man or woman who has a testimony of this work has no fear for the future. Come what may, they will look up and forward. We need the gospel of Jesus Christ in this world. We have it and through us it can be given to others to bless them.

"Be united. Be prayerful. Love one another. Husbands, love your wives. Children, love your parents. Remember God in all your activities and seek his counsel and guidance in all your undertakings.

"May you be blessed with leaders who believe in Jesus Christ and are willing to enthrone his principles of conduct in their public and private administration of office. I pray that your faith and prayers will be directed toward the Father that he may bless your leaders with the necessary wisdom, patience and courage to restore your nation as a blessing to freedom-loving people everywhere. Above all I pray that the way may remain open for the preaching of the gospel among your fellow countrymen. I am confident that there are thousands who will accept this glad message and live by it even as you are doing.

"I know as I know that I live that Jesus is the Christ, the Redeemer of mankind, the Savior of the world. I know that God our Eternal Father lives, that he speaks to his prophets today and that we are all literally his sons and daughters in the spirit and may become such in fuller measure throughout the eternities if we will accept the gospel, live it and merit fellowship with him in the celestial kingdom. I have seen this power; I have felt it in my life. Since becoming a member of the Council of the Twelve Apostles I have seen this power made manifest more strongly than ever before in my life.

"God is at the helm. He is leading us. He will not permit his Church and kingdom to fail. God has given us this assurance from the heavens. This is his work. May he help us to cherish his teachings and to live by them.... I bless you that you may always have a love for the truth. And I promise you, as a servant of the Lord, that if you are true and faithful, you shall not be denied any blessing of which you are worthy, even though for the present you are not able to enjoy fully the blessings which his children may receive in his holy temples. But I can assure you that he will make these blessings up to you in his own way, for your righteous desires are known by him and you shall yet be given an opportunity to express them fully."

President Benson's message touched every heart. Brother Max Zimmer served as interpreter and did a masterful job. I was so engrossed in what was being said and in watching the faces of those in the audience that my notes were incomplete, but the spirit of that occasion made an indelible impression upon my soul. Seldom have I felt so strongly the presence of the Divine Power.

After the meeting, President Benson stood at the rear of the meetinghall and shook hands personally with each person present. Expressions of faith and devotion lighted their faces as they felt his warmth and sincere love for them. Some of these good people returned to the line a second and even a third time so that they might shake his hand again and be strengthened by his radiant spirit of love and compassion.

While this was proceeding, President Zimmer pointed out to me a somewhat timid and emaciated sister. She had burlap sacks wrapped around her feet and legs in place of shoes. Even these were now in shreds. Her clothing was patched and tattered. As I looked at her purple-gray face, her swollen red eyes and protruding joints, I was told that I was looking at a person in the advanced stages of starvation. President Zimmer acquainted me with her hardships and incredible testimony.

This good sister had lived in East Prussia. During the final days of the frightful battles in that area, her husband had been killed. She was left with four small children, one of them a babe in arms. Under the agreements of the occupying military powers, she was one of 11 million Germans who was required to leave her homeland and all her basic possessions, and go to Western Germany to seek a new home. She was permitted only to take such bare necessities, bedding, etc. as she could load into her small wooden-wheeled wagon—about sixty-five pounds in all—

which she pulled across this desolate wasteland of war. Her smallest child she carried in her arms while the other small children did their best to walk beside her during this trek of over a thousand miles on foot.

She started her journey in late summer. Having neither food nor money among her few possessions, she was forced to gather a daily subsistence from the fields and forests along the way. Constantly she was also faced with dangers from panicky refugees and marauding troops.

Soon the snows came and temperatures dropped to about 40° below zero. One by one her children died, either frozen to death or the victims of starvation, or both. She buried them in shallow graves by the roadside, using a tablespoon as a shovel. Finally, as she was reaching the end of her journey, her last little child died in her arms. Her spoon was gone now, so she dug a grave in the frozen earth with her bare fingers.

As she was recalling these and other difficulties at a testimony meeting, she explained that her grief at that moment became unbearable. Here she was kneeling in the snow at the graveside of her last child. She had now lost her husband and all her children. She had given up all her earthly goods, her home, and even her homeland. She found herself among people whose condition resembled her own wretched state of affairs.

In this moment of deep sorrow and bewilderment, she felt her heart would break. In despair she contemplated how she might end her own life as so many of her fellow countrymen were doing. How easy it would be to jump off a nearby bridge, she thought, or to throw herself in front of an oncoming train!

Then she testified that as these thoughts assailed her, something within her said, "Get down on your knees and pray." And she then rapturously explained how she prayed more fervently than she had ever prayed before.

In conclusion, she bore a glorious testimony, stating that of all ailing people in her saddened land she was one of the happiest because she knew that God lived, that Jesus is the Christ, and that if she continued faithful and true to the end she would be saved in the celestial kingdom of God.

As the impact of this good sister's experience bore in upon

my soul, I felt to cry out against my own ingratitude. "But for the grace of God," thought I, "this might have been my own story. How thankful I am that my parents accepted the gospel as young people and braved the hardships which confronted them in going to the United States." I had never felt more grateful for my own wonderful parents.

Brother Badger arranged for us to eat breakfast with the military officers the next morning. It was a simple but nourishing meal. I could not help notice how many meals were only half eaten. To see food wantonly wasted in the midst of abject hunger seemed bordering on the unforgivable. Many in the neighborhood would have been overjoyed to receive a small portion of what was being thrown away each day in this military unit.

As we reentered Switzerland, I was startled by the extreme contrast with what we had just seen and experienced. Here is a land of clean beauty. Wherever one looks he sees everything immaculately kept. The rolling hills, peaceful green valleys, sparkling mountain streams, picturesque waterfalls and majestic snow-covered Alps all blend together to make Switzerland a veritable paradise.

Basel, the site of our mission headquarters, is a charming city on the Rhine river right at the point where the French and German borders touch Switzerland. This is a city of long standing. As early as 374 A.D. Roman army accounts referred to it as Camp Basilea. The Rhine river is navigable from its mouth to Basel, so this provides a direct sea outlet. The people take pride in being industrious and, for the benefit of Americans, they reminded us that one of Basel's citizens was General John August Sutter of California fame.

Before returning to Germany, we visited the Swiss capital of Berne and then drove to Geneva, both visits being made in the interest of getting supplies and materials to meet pressing needs for our saints until our welfare shipments could begin to arrive in substantial volume. We succeeded in authorizing an initial carload of food to be shipped to Berlin to meet the critical needs of our refugee saints arriving there. The International Red Cross and all other offices contacted pledged to assist us to the extent possible under the then existing military and governmental restrictions.

When we left to reenter Germany, our car was loaded with as many items of food as we could crowd in and still leave enough room for the four of us to be sandwiched in like sardines. Fortunately we were cleared by the Swiss and French border officials without having to surrender any of these items.

Anticipating our arrival in Freiburg, the good saints had assembled themselves at the home of their branch president. They were overjoyed to see and talk with us, even though our stay had to be brief. While there we administered to a wretched-looking brother who had just returned from three years as a prisoner of war among the French. He was physically on the verge of complete collapse as a result of starvation and felt that, since most of the people in the French zone could not get more than 350 calories of foodstuffs a day, only the power of God could preserve him and restore him to health. As President Benson finished blessing this good man, all of us expressed the determination to do our utmost in finding ways to get the welfare supplies to those people in the shortest possible time.

As we drove along, we passed portions of the Siegfried Line. Some of these heavily reinforced steel and concrete bunkers were nearly demolished, while others were actually split in two. Near the outskirts of Heidelberg was a large garbage dump where army trucks deposited their refuse. We stopped in amazement to see the hordes of people—ranging in age from small toddling children to elderly grandparents—scrounging to salvage whatever they might find of useful food, clothing, etc. It was a sickening sight to witness. President Zimmer had loaded his pockets with Swiss candies before we left, and when he started giving some to a few of the children near our car, we suddenly found ourselves almost overpowered by the swarm of people coming toward us from all directions. In self-defense we had to move away quickly.

The closer we came to Frankfurt, the more intensive the bombing appeared to have been. Before we reached our destination, we were thoroughly shocked and appalled by what we had seen and experienced. Frankfurt, while not listed among the worst-bombed cities in Germany, was a sickening shambles. It had been 65 percent to 70 percent destroyed. All of its bridges had been blasted or dynamited. Some had been trussed up with wooden sections to permit traffic to pass over them, while others were hopelessly beyond repair. The old cathedral spire still remained standing, but everything flammable had been destroyed. The opera house and beautiful civic center lay in ruins. Zeilstrasse, once the "Fifth Avenue" of Frankfurt, was nothing but a ghost street of crumbling walls and twisted steel.

The mission home was still standing and was reasonably serviceable. It had suffered from several near bomb hits, but had escaped miraculously from a "blockbuster" which fell in the courtyard but failed to explode. The mere impact of this bomb burying itself into the ground cracked some of the walls. Had this bomb exploded, all of our mission office personnel and all the mission records would have been completely wiped out.

The most severe damage to the mission home had resulted from the dynamiting of the Adolf Hitler Bridge, just across the street from the home. We were told that the retreating Germans had had to make eight detonations to make the bridge impassable.

Our LDS servicemen had anticipated our arrival and had already laid the groundwork so that we might arrange for military passes to the Army Officers' Mess Hall and for sleeping accommodations at the Carlton Hotel, which the Army had partially repaired in order to provide quarters for traveling military and governmental personnel.

After a welcome breakfast, we drove to the United States Forces, European Theater (USFET), headquarters, housed in the beautiful I. G. Farben building in Frankfurt. This building, we were told, was spared from bombing by the Allied airmen in anticipation of its use as a future military headquarters for our forces.

We proceeded to the offices of General Joseph T. McNarney, the four-star general in charge of all American forces in Europe. Our first request for an audience was quickly and routinely dismissed. The general's aide, a very businesslike major, advised us that it would be impossible to arrange such a meeting for at least three days.

Somewhat disappointed, we returned to our car where President Benson suggested that we unite our faith in petitioning the Lord. He humbly asked the Lord to be mindful of our situation and to open the way before us.

When we returned to General McNarney's office several minutes later, we were greeted by another officer who was apparently relieving the major Without mentioning our earlier contact with the major, President Benson requested an audience with the general. This aide agreed to place in his hands a special letter of introduction from Senator Elbert D. Thomas, Chairman of the powerful Senate Committee on Military Affairs. Within fifteen minutes we were ushered in for a meeting with the general.

As we entered, it was evident that he regarded this interview as strictly a perfunctory one which he was anxious to terminate as quickly as possible so that he might get on with more pressing matters. President Benson warmly shook his hand and stood there looking squarely at him and talking very earnestly. This was a crucial moment. So much of our future success seemed to hang on the outcome of this interview.

At first the general seemed visibly annoyed. When he heard of our proposed itinerary through all four military zones of occupation in Germany and Austria, as well as entrance into Czechoslovakia, he looked startled that we would even consider such an ambitious undertaking under the then-existing restricted conditions. President Benson continued to gaze intently into the general's eyes as he talked with him, and he spoke with such feeling and conviction that the general's eyes became moist with tears and his cold militaristic manner gave way to a warm, spirited expression of, "Mr. Benson, there's something about you that I like. I want to help you in every way that I can!"

I could not help but recall the promise made to President Benson in his letter of appointment. At that time the First Presidency wrote:

> "...Your influence [will] be felt for good by all you come in contact with, and...you and they [will] be made to feel that there is a power and spirit accompanying you not of man."

As President Benson explained the nature of our mission and the organization of the Church and its welfare program, General McNarney exclaimed, "Mr. Benson, I have never heard of a church with such vision!"

The general then advised us that for the present time regulations required that all relief supplies be handled and distributed through military channels. However, as he became acquainted with our mission organization and our ability to make our own distribution equitably, he continued to express his amazement. Finally he volunteered that perhaps they might change the regulations in the near future to accommodate us. Meanwhile he suggested that we begin to gather our relief supplies.

When President Benson informed him that we had ninety large welfare storehouses bulging with food and clothing, which could be ready for shipment within twenty-four hours, one could fairly feel the general's astonishment. He then agreed to give us written authorization to make our own distribution through our own channels. In exchange, we agreed to provide a reasonable amount of our foodstuffs for use in the existing child-feeding program.

After this point was reached, General McNarney seemed willing to consider favorably our every request. He reminded us that we would be the first American civilians to make the trip to Berlin by car since the military occupation and said he did not feel that the military could accept responsibility for our safe passage through the Russian Zone, inasmuch as the military itself had suffered unexplained disappearances of military equipment and personnel on the highway to Berlin recently.

When President Benson assured him that we were not fearful for our personal safety and did not expect such guarantee for our safety, he seemed relieved and agreed to provide us with the necessary military orders to assure us of limited use of military facilities throughout our travels. He also dictated a letter of introduction to General Lucius Clay, who was in charge of the Office of Military Government, United States (OMGUS), in Berlin. This proved to be of considerable help in arranging for pertinent conferences upon our arrival.

While we were dining at the officers' mess in Frankfurt, a spirited string ensemble was playing sweet music. The leader of the group approached our table and asked if we had any special request. President Benson said we would like to hear them play "When It's Springtime in the Rockies." The leader being unfamiliar with this song, President Benson hummed the tune to him, whereupon he returned to his gifted companions, hummed the tune to them, then led them in playing the song beautifully and with scarcely a mistake. This performance pleased our group very much.

We later learned that these fine musicians played all evening in exchange for a meal and whatever extra gifts those present might give them.

Later in the day we drove out to Langen (near Frankfurt) and called on Mr. P. Moderegger, whose wife was a member of the Church. He operated a large fruit and vegetable nursery and had offered to let some of our refugee saints from the East house themselves upon his property. This provided work for many of them. We reviewed the situation with him and worked out arrangements whereby an additional twenty-five families could be cared for there. Over thirty of our saints were already living there at that time.

President Benson expressed concern over the condition of the mission records. Wartime conditions made it virtually impossible to keep an accurate accounting of memberships and events, although a fairly good ledger was kept for listing income and expenses. To convert the mass of disorganized information into seven years of accurate and acceptable records and accounts proved to be a staggering assignment, since we found comparable situations in all the missions of Europe and had to institute the same action in each of them. Yet before the first year came to an end, the entire task had been successfully completed.

One of the critical problems was how to arrange some place for our many saints to stay who were fleeing from the Polish territories as refugees to Berlin. Many were arriving without food or adequate clothing, and some were trudging through the winter snows barefooted. Some of these refugees were dying in spite of all efforts being made to care for them. Two temporary projects for their relief were being supervised by the mission presidency in Berlin, but the large number of arrivals rendered these facilities woefully inadequate.

To help alleviate this condition, while he was in Switzerland, President Benson arranged for the purchase of some Swiss military barracks. These were quickly dismantled and shipped on military trucks to the areas in greatest need. At the time such arrangements seemed incredible, not only to the saints but also to our military personnel who were familiar with existing shortages and restrictions. It was but another evidence of how the Lord prepared the way before us to achieve his purposes.

A week previously, a baptismal service had been conducted at Bielefeld at which eleven new members were added to the Church. It was necessary to cut a large hole through the ice on the river to serve as a baptismal font. In spite of their weakened physical condition, none of the participants suffered any ill effects. Eleven additional baptisms had taken place in Karlsruhe the previous day, we were advised.

At that time the official daily food ration in the French Zone of occupation was 400 to 500 calories. One group of saints living there had been unable for several weeks to obtain any kind of bread to use as one of the sacramental emblems. They were so anxious to partake of the sacrament that they purchased some potato peelings which cost fifty dollars and used these in place of bread. President Benson, upon learning of this circumstance, suggested that the Lord was probably pleased to accept of their offering, since he had revealed to the Church that it did not matter what emblems were used so long as they were blessed and partaken for the renewing of the sacred covenants.

During the war years some of our saints lost their lives, while others were scarred or maimed for life. Our mission secretary, Sister Ilse Bruenger Foerster, was one of the latter. She had to bear the brunt of brutal Gestapo investigations and several merciless beatings In addition, she had to carry the major load at times for day-to-day mission affairs.

Charges were leveled that she was sending mission funds to

America. After two weeks of grueling interrogations, beatings, and constant surveillance, during which time many mission records were confiscated and some of them destroyed, she was released with the threat that not only her own life but the lives of members of her family and relatives would stand in jeopardy if she ever revealed the nature of her questioning. During this critical time she was expecting her first child, but in spite of such threats and the terrific strain imposed upon her, she successfully denied every false charge and refuted every accusation. Her accusers marveled at her intense faith and her devotion to the Church. When questioned about how she was able to bear up under these trials, she answered simply that she had always placed her complete trust in the Lord and that he had always sustained her through every circumstance.

Several days before we arrived in Frankfurt, three German prisoners of war, who had just been released from a prisoner-of-war camp near Ogden, Utah, entered the local employment placement agency where Sister Foerster was employed as a translator. One of these men was a former doctor, another a former dentist, and the third a former architect. While filling out their questionnaires, they distributed tracts and books to the employees. Then they addressed the group, stating that they had received this literature while at the prison camp in America and that they felt they had at last found the truth.

They explained that they had not only studied and learned of its teachings, but that they had seen the wonderful results in the lives of the members of the church among whom they had been living as prisoners of war. They added that although they were not yet members of this church, they felt an obligation to tell others of the great happiness that had come into their lives.

Of course, the tracts they had passed out were Mormon tracts and the books were copies of the Book of Mormon!

While working on the mission records, I inquired about the large bomb that had fallen in the courtyard of the mission home without exploding. I was given the following details:

The mission staff could hear the approaching planes dropping bombs block by block and could sense the approaching doom. Only sisters were in the home that day, and they all hurried to the basement, where they knelt in a prayer circle, pleading with the Lord to spare their lives, but wondering whether each moment would be their last. They heard the terrific explosion in the block just next to them. Then they heard and felt the tremendous thud of the "blockbuster" bomb, but it did not explode. It landed in the courtyard with such force that windows were shattered and some of the walls were cracked. The next bomb fell with deadly precision in the next block and leveled it to the ground. Before this raid was completed, most of the homes and offices on their side of the river were left pulverized and burning. These sisters had miraculously escaped to tell their story.

At the time I could not help but recall how Sister Edith Longbone of the British Mission staff had related to me a few days earlier a parallel experience. It seems that she was living near the white cliffs of Dover during the war. This area was subjected to repeated shellings and bombings, including the infamous V-2 rockets. During all these hectic days, she invited many of her neighbors to come into her home during the bombings and shellings rather than retreating to air-raid shelters. Said she, "I've had my home dedicated by a servant of the Lord and no harm shall come to it." Her faith was vindicated and she survived with many grateful neighbors and friends.

The German saints at this time were in a seriously scattered condition. This made active Church attendance and participation difficult, but their faithfulness was nonetheless amazing. Nearly all meetinghouses had been destroyed. Many branches were meeting in the homes of the relatively few members who still could claim a home of their own—between 80 percent and 85 percent of the total German membership had been bombed out of their homes repeatedly or had lost them altogether.

When President Benson outlined what steps had been taken and what was planned for the future, one could sense the flame of faith and perseverance being rekindled in the membership.

We learned that our branch in Pforzheim was virtually wiped out. During the war years considerable dissension had arisen among the members, and this mounted until it was found necessary to discontinue meetings altogether. Since their city was a costume jewelry center rather than a prime military target, the people of Pforzheim felt reasonably secure Each time military planes flew overhead, however, on their way to military targets to the south and east, the people would seek the added protection of their air-raid shelters.

After one particular bombing group had passed them by and the "all-clear" had been sounded, the people returned to their normal duties. Then without warning the bombs began to fall. Apparently the British attacking force had encountered heavy German fighter opposition and had been unable to deliver their bombs on target. Lightening their planes in an effort to reach the safety of their own shores, they unloaded their entire bomb-load on this unsuspecting city. The city was left 95 percent demolished. As far as was known, only one family of Church members had escaped the onslaught.

We were assured that where unity prevailed, most of our people suffered far fewer casualties. An example was related to us wherein one branch continued holding their services in spite of frequent air raids. The only time a meeting was dismissed early was the day the American soldiers arrived. Among arriving American servicemen there were always some members of the Church, and these always gave what help they could. Our LDS servicemen were held in the highest esteem everywhere we traveled.

While in Germany, President Benson instructed our leaders to compile the names and addresses of all mission, district and branch officers and teachers and submit these lists to the denazification courts. This was done. In all the investigations which followed, not a single one of these people was considered to be guilty of punishable crimes—a remarkable record!

Before continuing our journey on to Berlin, President Benson addressed a large group of saints on Sunday and left them with these challenging words ringing in their ears:

"So long as you are true and faithful and live the gospel, you will never lose your testimony of the divinity of this work and the transcendent mission of Jesus Christ. All experiences that may come into your lives shall be made sweet unto you in the Lord's own due time and you shall yet be saved in the celestial kingdom of God, which is to be an heir of the greatest of all the gifts of God to man."

It was heartening to see and feel the intense concern our servicemen had for our welfare. They knew all too well the almost insurmountable tasks we faced, but from the blessings we had already received, we felt assured that we would accomplish all that the Lord would have us do. As for our safety, I had the divine assurance that we would not be harmed; consequently, worry and fear were complete strangers to me. I did exhibit some native curiosity from time to time, however, in wondering just how our task would be accomplished.

En route to Berlin we remained overnight in Hannover to meet with district and branch presidents from the British Zone of occupation. We found this city to be in even worse condition than Frankfurt. In the course of our meeting, we learned how seriously our members had suffered as a result of the war. We met in the home of Brother Pohlsander, Hannover District President. Most of those present were quite emaciated and their clothing hung loosely from their shoulders. There were none who did not have to cinch in their belts.

We were advised that in some of the larger branches the destruction had been so complete that they didn't even have a single Bible left by the end of hostilities. They had relied completely upon divine guidance, with the result that we found them sound in doctrine and in faith.

Arrangements were hurriedly made to hold an evening meeting with the saints in a room of a bombed-out schoolhouse. There was no electricity. When we arrived at dusk, we found the room overflowing with assembled saints. The most impressive thing to me was to see ten or twelve children on each side of the center aisle standing on chairs. As we proceeded down the aisle to take our seats at the front of the room, they scattered armloads of gorgeous flowers in our pathway and created a living carpet of indescribable beauty. What a glorious way to welcome an apostle of the Lord! President Benson and all of us were moved to tears of overwhelming gratitude for this marvelous demonstration of pure love. It was with great difficulty that any of us could suppress our tender emotions sufficiently to speak and otherwise take part in the meeting which followed.

All the window panes had been shattered by repeated bombings and had been replaced with sections of cardboard nailed or otherwise held in place. The windows were now opened wide to admit the fading daylight. We had barely begun our meeting when a violent rain and windstorm broke out. This necessitated quickly closing all the windows and continuing our services in almost total darkness. In spite of this condition, the hastily formed choir, which I had been invited to join, sang fervently, even though we could barely see our director.

The meeting opened with the singing of "We Thank Thee, O God, for a Prophet." And how they sang that song! After President Benson's stirring remarks (it was too dark to make any notes), the choir appropriately sang, "Come, O Thou King of Kings." I believe the very heavens were moved by the spirited singing.

chapter four

Hardships Unlimited

We had heard all kinds of stories about the "terrible" Russians, but when we actually reached the Russian Zone border station at Helmstedt we were pleasantly surprised that we received permission to go on without undue difficulty. The guards seemed surprised to see us and our peculiar looking car. We had painted large "US" letters on each fender before leaving Hannover. (They might have wondered why we hadn't spelled out USSR!) We could not converse with them, since they could speak no English, German or French, but after they checked our credentials and military orders, which had been furnished us in Frankfurt before we left, they seemed to be satisfied. They said "Dobra" (or something like that), and waved for us to go on.

Except for the numerous detours until we had reached the Russian and American checkpoints at the outskirts of Berlin, our trip was most enjoyable.

For the first time the four of us traveling together (President Benson, President Zimmer, Chaplain Badger, and myself) formed a male quartet. We sang all the songs we knew to make the time pass more quickly and pleasantly. President Benson sang melody, President Zimmer the high tenor, Chaplain Badger the bass, and I filled in with the tenor or baritone part as needed. We nicknamed ourselves the "K-Ration Quartet," since we were subsisting largely on K-rations during our entire trip. Frequently we were asked how we enjoyed this kind of diet, to which President Benson always replied, "They are nutritious, but monotonous!"

The American guards at "Checkpoint Charlie" in Berlin

were surprised to see us and our unusually-decorated car, but were most cordial in welcoming us to this "free" city.

The once-magnificent city of Berlin was an indescribable scene of desolation and destruction. Probably not a single house, we were told, had escaped without considerable damage. It was evident that the houses on some streets had been repaired sufficiently to provide some living quarters. I couldn't believe my eyes as we drove down many of the once-famous streets. The feelings of grief and incredulity were so overwhelming that we could scarcely speak and were almost tempted to close our eyes to shut out what we saw.

Evidence on all sides assured us that the people were beginning to uncover and bury their dead, to remove the rubble as rapidly as their weakened bodies would permit, and to forge ahead in the hope that Berlin would one day rise again.

The beautiful Tiergarten—once considered to be one of the world's largest, most luxuriant and beautifully kept parks—was nothing but a far-flung mass of broken tree stumps, shattered monuments, and fearsome-looking bunkers standing silently as grim reminders of this, the most destructive of all wars to date.

The following day Lieutenant General Lucius D. Clay, Deputy Governor of OMGUS, reviewed the problems of the Church in carrying on general relief and rehabilitation activities as well as proselyting functions. He pledged his full cooperation, as requested by General McNarney, and expressed his appreciation for having the Church on the job in the Occupied Areas ready to help with the mammoth job of rehabilitation both materially and spiritually.

The Berlin representative of the International Red Cross, Dr. A. R. Lindt, assured us that his organization was prepared to receive welfare shipments we had purchased while in Switzerland and would turn them over to our mission authorities upon their arrival, although they would have to be distributed in Berlin rather than in the Russian Zone, which was still barred to such assistance.

Earlier we had seen some of the destruction in the Western

sectors of this sprawling city, but as we toured the Russian Sector with some of our servicemen that evening, we saw what was incredible. An effort was being made in the sectors we had visited earlier to clean up and rebuild, but in the Russian Sector there was a total feeling of stagnation, hopelessness, and stalking death. One had to experience it personally to begin to appreciate the profound difference. And the pervading stench of decaying human bodies made the scenes we witnessed all the more oppressive and overpowering in their spirit of abject hopelessness that seemed to be everywhere present.

In Berlin we visited the mission headquarters, a newly rented place which had been the former home of a high Nazi official. The grounds around the house were spruced up by a German member of the Church for the occasion of President Benson's visit. Little could be done with the building itself. All window panes were shattered. Bleak shutters remained to cover the window openings. The roof, however, appeared to be in fair condition.

We were met at the mission headquarters by Acting Mission President Richard Ranglak, and his first counselor, Paul Langheinrich. As President Benson was shown through the home, he was overwhelmed by the sight of many heavy volumes of church records in German stacked three to four feet high in the spacious rooms on the first floor. Then he learned of what was perhaps the most remarkable activity of these German brethren during the entire war period.

In 1938 and 1939 the Genealogical Society of Utah tried without success to make arrangements for buying microfilms of genealogical records from the German government. After the missionaries were evacuated, Brother Langheinrich, as mission genealogical leader, made arrangements for the German government to construct a microfilming machine for use of the Church. The machine was finished, but war between Germany and the United States terminated further work

Brother Langheinrich watched developments closely and after war had ended he wrote a letter on August 9, 1945, to

Russian Field Marshall Zhukoff, Russian commander of the East Zone of Germany at Karlshorst in East Berlin, asking for permission to provide foodstuffs for our suffering refugee saints and also for permission to search for all genealogical records and films in this territory. Permission was granted.

(This permission, secured with the aid of the International Red Cross, enabled us to make distribution in the Russian Sector of Berlin. Since this sector had free access to East Germany, limited supplies were now made available to our refugee camps located there. We were not free to make a wider distribution until final permission was given by the Russian authorities during the last week of my mission.)

After long searching for these records, two large groups were discovered in the Rothenburg and Rathsfeld castles in the mountains of Thuringia Additional precious records had been located in some nearby salt mines in the mountains. The first discoveries netted six to seven thousand church books, photocopies of most of these books, and about five thousand rolls of microfilm. This carload of records was moved to our mission office.

Two days before our arrival a much larger store of records was found in a salt mine in Thuringia—nearly three carloads—among which were many East Prussian records. It was estimated that there were over 140 boxes of microfilm rolls, which could possibly contain over 100 million names. The entire record group weighed about 25 tons. In addition, there were 60 boxes of church records, 30 boxes of card indexes, 15,000 packages of church books, 15,000 photocopies of books, and many other items. We noticed that in these piles were many Jewish records as well as Catholic church registers. Very few of them had suffered any appreciable damage.

Brother Langheinrich related to me the amazing story of how they were able to bring down the records from the mountain on which Rothenburg castle is located. A Russian official had promised him a German railway car at a nearby siding into which these records could be loaded for shipment to Berlin. Brother Langheinrich went to the castle with sixteen missionaries to haul these records down the mountainside to the railway car at the siding. Two of the brethren went nearby to secure a truck while the rest went to the castle to get these records prepared for shipment. They waited a long time, but no truck arrived. Finally it was reported that the truck could not drive up the mountain road which was covered with ice. This was critical. The railway car was due shortly and had to be loaded within a couple of hours, so it was vital that these records be brought down to the valley below.

Brother Langheinrich and three of the brethren retired to a nearby wooded section and called upon the Lord in prayer. They explained the urgency of their need for assistance and asked for his help. As they said "Amen," the truck arrived, but without the trailer they had expected to use. However, even though the road was slippery, they succeeded in getting the records safely to the railway car at the siding.

Then they had to get some additional records from a second castle nearby. They felt that the only way they could get these records would be to have a warm rain that night to melt the ice on the mountain road. Although it had been freezing, there was a sudden change, warm rain fell during the night, and they were able to bring down all the records which we now saw before us. Right after the records were recovered, a heavy snow began to fall and the road was frozen over again.

Thus we were able to bring all of these records together and eventually turn them over to the East German authorities in first-class condition. They were later placed in the East German National Archives, where they may eventually be made available for the use of researchers and historians.

Later in the day we visited the site of our former mission home at Haendelallee 6 and Brother Langheinrich's home on Rathenowerstrasse. When we arrived at the former mission home, we were greeted by all that remained—a small section of the wall where the bay window used to be. This was only about three feet high.

So complete had been the destruction of the heavily forested Tiergarten adjacent to the mission home, that I could look for miles in all directions with scarcely a single obstruction to hinder my view. It was impossible for me to imagine that such complete desolation could ever exist anywhere upon the earth. I felt heart-sick and my very soul was weeping.

As we were driving over to see Brother Langheinrich's home, he told us of the night this mission home had been destroyed. One of our fine servicemen, Brother Don C. Corbett, who was with us, had written about this tragedy earlier in such inspiring terms that I persuaded him to make a copy of his account available to me so that I might record the facts more accurately. His account was as follows:

> During the night of November 22, 1943, Berlin received heavy bombing attack. More than 1,000 planes based in England took part. All the houses around the East German Mission home were destroyed. The neighborhood around Brother Paul Langheinrich's home at 52 Rathenower Strasse was heavily damaged and burned. The next morning the windows of the mission home were found to be broken. The roof and ceiling were damaged. The office workers cleaned up the glass and repaired the roof the best they could.

> Then about midday, according to Paul Langheinrich, he heard a whispering within: "Bring all the sisters out of the home immediately." At the time there were four lady missionaries quartered in the building. He told them to pack their things and prepare to move their trunks. With their belongings, the sisters evacuated the mission headquarters and moved to the home of Brother Langheinrich.

> Two or three hours later, Brother Herbert Klopfer (acting mission president), home on leave from the Russian front, arrived at the mission home with his wife. He found the place locked. He wanted to get in but had forgotten the key. He left to find Brother Richard Ranglak, who was acting mission leader in his stead A few minutes later the bombers came again A direct hit by a 500-pound bomb completely destroyed the home, leaving it a mass of rubble. Because of the whisperings of the Spirit however, not a single life of our mission staff was lost.

During our first Sunday in Berlin, we met in the Russian Sector in a badly damaged schoolhouse with 480 friends and members. It was a time of great rejoicing. Again Brother

Corbett's description of this event relates in a beautiful manner what transpired:

> The German saints were in their places when Elder Benson arrived. They all stood up when he entered and made his way to the stand. It was a wonderful sight to look into their faces and to feel their spirit of devotion and gratitude. An air of great expectancy was there as well as a certain tenseness. Everyone anxiously awaited for the servant of the Lord to commence speaking. There was also a note of sadness. As the eye took in the scene and beheld the emaciated faces, etched with sorrow and tragedy, a feeling of sympathy was kindled for them. Many were suffering from advanced stages of malnutrition. Some were in great need of medical care. On this day, however, their spiritual desires transcended their temporal wants. These were the faithful, the backbone of the Church in Berlin, but many of them needed encouragement and needed light and guidance to set their thinking straight.
>
> President Benson arose, with Brother Zimmer as interpreter.... When he had finished, everyone present realized that he had spoken under the direction of the Spirit of God. His voice was choked with emotion as he started, but gradually took on vigor and power. The climax seemed to be reached when he caused heads to bow with these ringing words: "When a nation follows unrighteous leaders, the righteous must suffer with the wicked."

As we were shaking hands with many of the people after the meeting, one little old sister came up to me and asked, "Do you remember me?" I looked at her carefully for a few moments and then replied, "Why, yes. You are Sister Labeda Freitag."

She seemed pleased that I remembered her. She was a member of the Schoeneberg Branch (now in the Russian Sector of Berlin) before the war.

"I am wondering if you remember the speech you made here just before Christmas in 1937," she asked.

My mind raced back and I thought I knew what she meant. Then she continued: "Just in case you don't remember, I wrote down some of your remarks at that time and have kept them right here in my little black notebook. At that time you challenged us to lead the Church in preparing our genealogical records. Then you made a promise and prophecy—let me read it to you—that if we proved our sincerity and faith, given ten years of peace in which to work, the Lord would bless us with a temple in Europe where we might receive our own sealings and endowments. Now I wish to ask you, Were you speaking under inspiration at that time? Will this promise be fulfilled?"

"How much time do we have left?" I asked.

"About eight years," she replied.

"If I spoke under the spirit of revelation," I continued, "you will see this promise fulfilled in full measure. If this does not happen, you will know that my remarks were not directed by the Lord." She seemed satisfied to bide her time.

(When the Swiss Temple was being constructed within this ten-year period, I was one of the most grateful members in the Church!)

We observed that, during and after the meeting, not a single member registered any complaint about his circumstances in spite of the fact that some were obviously in the last stages of starvation. In Berlin alone, we were told the pervading attitude of hopelessness caused over a hundred suicides daily. Our saints, on the other hand, were full of hope, courage, and faith. Everywhere we met with them they reflected a quiet optimism and a spirit of gratitude for the Church and the gospel of Jesus Christ.

As we knelt together in prayer that night, President Benson poured out his soul to the Lord in behalf of these wonderful people. We realized the stringent conditions under which they had to live We could not doubt, however, that they would be equal to the challenge, for we had witnessed a measure of faith that rarely has had its equal.

After seventeen long hours of most difficult driving, we arrived in Nuremberg, where the War Crime Trials were being held. The old city was considered by many to be the worst-bombed and devastated city in the entire nation. Not a single building remained standing. Many of the streets were still hopelessly blocked with rubble and bomb craters. Both of our meetinghouses had been completely destroyed. Almost without exception, members had been bombed or burned out of their homes one or more times.

Darkness had enveloped the city long before our arrival. With extreme difficulty we finally found the old bombed-out schoolhouse where the saints were meeting under very adverse circumstances, particularly since there were no street lights and virtually no lights in the entire area.

One little light illuminated the meetingroom. One wall was missing and a cold breeze and light snow added to the discomfort of this unheated building. The two hundred shivering saints had begun their meeting at 7:30, and in spite of a curfew requiring all German civilians to be off the streets at 10 p.m. they had decided to remain here until we arrived.

President Benson suggested the possibility of concluding the meeting without speaking to them so that they might reach their homes in the few minutes remaining before the curfew, but they called out almost as one voice: "Speak to us. We will remain right here overnight!"

After the benediction one sister came up to me and asked, "Do you remember me?"

I looked searchingly at her and then replied, "You are Sister Frenzel."

She confirmed this, then continued: "Do you remember the promises you made to me when you blessed me just before you left Nuremberg in 1939 to return home?"

How could I ever forget! I had given my farewell talk in church. Then, by request, I went to her home to give her a blessing. She was expecting her first child. Her health was so poor that she had been unable to come to church except on rare occasions. Because of serious physical complications and the fact that she was in her forties while expecting this, her first child, the family doctor had expressed grave concern that she might lose her own life in giving birth to a child.

In view of these problems she had asked for a special blessing.

Her husband was a cripple with one leg. They were poor people and lived in a little shed on their "Gartenlaube." This shed was ordinarily used to store garden tools, etc., for taking care of this little piece of land on which they might grow a few fruits and vegetables. Because of their meager circumstances, they had converted this into a one-room home. And under such circumstances the arrival of a child would be even more critical.

In the middle of the blessing I stopped, completely bewildered by the fact that I had blessed her that She would have a son. Knowing how literally these good people accepted every word of the elders, I was concerned that I had committed a serious mistake.

My companion nudged me to go on. As I did so, I tried to think of how I could possibly word the blessing to make this a conditional promise. Then I realized that I had just said for a second time that her child should grow up to receive the priesthood and become a leader in the Church. At this point I recognized that I had left no room for retreat, so I resolved to continue the blessing and get through it as best I could.

To make matters even worse, as the blessing continued I promised her that she should have no serious pain in childbirth (yet the doctor feared for her very life) and that because of her faith she should yet rear a large family (this, too, was impossible, according to the doctor who marveled that she could expect even one child because of her age).

When the blessing had been concluded, she smiled and said, in effect, that she knew she would be all right, that she would have a son and that the Lord would bless and sustain her. Yes, how well I remember that blessing!

On my way home that evening, even the mission president had offered me no consolation. As I recounted the circumstances to him, he merely said, "You have a fifty-fifty chance of being right!"

It was now nearly seven years later. After my vivid, split-second review, Sister Frenzel said to me, "I would like to have you meet my family." She then paraded her little ones before me—four or five of them, as I recall—and introduced them. Her firstborn, a son, she had named Frederick William after me!

Another young man in the audience approached me a few moments later and asked, "Do you remember the promises you made to me when you blessed me just as I was entering the German army?"

Again I recalled the circumstances rather vividly, and

replied: "I believe I do. Why do you ask?"

"Because I have found the young woman I would like to marry. Do you think it is still possible for me to be married to her in the temple, as I was promised in that blessing?"

(I had promised him, according to his wishes, that if he lived a clean, pure life, the Lord would grant him the privilege of being married in the House of the Lord—a thing which seemed remote and impossible at that time when we were standing on the brink of the outbreak of World War II and he was going into the German infantry.)

As I looked upon his emaciated body—possibly weighing around 100 pounds instead of the 180 pounds or so he weighed when he entered the service—and realized the difficult circumstances under which he and many others lived, I became somewhat apprehensive. "Hans," I asked, "have you kept yourself morally clean since that day?"

"Yes, I have," he assured me. "I was severely wounded and left for dead on the battlefield more than once, but I have kept myself morally clean."

Then I was impressed to say: "Hans, if you have kept yourself clean and you still desire to make that promise a reality, claim your blessing from the Lord. I don't understand right now how it will be possible, but somehow the Lord will open the way."

(After I had returned home and was working in the Church office building in Salt Lake City, who should walk in one day but Hans and his sweetheart. They were being married in the Temple. They had arranged for a visitor's visa and were to return to their homeland after their marriage and a short stay in the United States. How they were able to get the finances together to make this nearly fifteen-thousand-mile round trip I do not know. I could not help marveling at the faith of that young man and his sweetheart.)

I would have loved to stay with those German saints overnight and to share with them a bed on the cold, bare, cement floor, but this was not possible and we had to take our leave.

chapter five

Faith Like the Ancients

As we entered Czechoslovakia, we enjoyed the sudden change of seeing villages almost untouched by the ravages of war. We saw store windows laden with goods (which many people could not buy because of rationing and lack of money), and horses and farm machinery working the land. It seemed like entering a new and better world.

I thought Prague a lovely city. Its many neon lights gave it the appearance of an American metropolitan city, except that the streets were more narrow and more crooked, and the lights were fewer.

We discovered that nearly all of the 115 members of the Czechoslovakian Mission had remained active in and faithful to the Church during the war. In spite of their small numbers, through their combined efforts they had been able to remain self-supporting as a mission. We found them carrying on a vigorous missionary proselyting program.

During the war the saints contributed toward a modest monument built on the spot where in 1929 Elder John A. Widtsoe of the Council of the Twelve dedicated this land to the preaching of the gospel. It was unveiled on July 24, 1945, just sixteen years after the date it commemorated.

We tried to get breakfast at a cafe. At first we were told that they could serve no food without ration stamps (of which we had none). With the aid of a package of American cigarettes, however, which we carried with us (at the suggestion of some of our servicemen) to meet just such emergencies, we were able to obtain a bounteous meal. It consisted of Linden blossom tea, bread and butter, caviar, fish, bologna, and a small piece of cake—a rather unusual breakfast, but very welcome.

Another package of cigarettes helped us to meet another crisis a few minutes later when we had two flat tires in quick succession. When I offered a generous sum of American money, my request for service was simply ignored. As soon as I showed some American cigarettes, the men let all their other work stand by while they quickly mended both tires.

Bad luck with tires continued to plague us. When the next tire blew out it was too late to get service, so we stayed overnight in Pilsen, the center of the large Skoda ammunition factory and the home of Europe's famous Pilsner beer.

This time Brother Zimmer became the bargaining agent. He had to give the chief clerk at the hotel some cigarettes so that arrangements could be made to get the ailing tire repaired early in the morning and thus not delay our departure. The man who did the actual work also had to be bribed. Then we had to repeat the process in order to get the hotel clerk to cash a travelers check for us. Without cigarettes, it seemed, these services were not available. (We were told unofficially that one carton of American cigarettes was considered as valuable as $4,000.00 in American money. Incredible!)

In a letter to my wife I reported the conditions we had faced:

> We've been going from 5 to 5:50 every morning until midnight or thereabouts.... Sometimes these long hours tire me out completely. The car is small, the roads are terribly rough, and the meals in the Occupied Zones are very meager. All in all we are really having it rough. If it aids, however, in getting welfare supplies to these people a day, a week, or a month sooner, and buoys them up in faith until shipments from America can arrive, I feel sure that many lives will be spared.

> It is a shame to see people—members of our Church—in the last stages of starvation, eyes bulging out, legs and ankles swelling, and becoming so listless that it is a major effort to speak. So far we haven't lost too many members as a result of starvation. Unofficially, we have had less than 100 so far, but unless something is done very soon, diseases and permanent

maladjustments due to faulty nutrition, etc., are sure to take a terrible toll.

Some families of three and four are living on what one person in the United States throws away. If a person hasn't enough money to pay fantastic prices illegally on the "black market" he must face starvation. If he deals on the "black market" he is not a loyal citizen and is liable to face fines or imprisonment, if caught.

The pace we are keeping is terrific. I hope we are able to slow down eventually. When one sees all the starving and suffering of these people, he is driven to work day and night.

At a meeting in Vienna we were happy to see the district president, Brother Alois Cziep, and Brother Franz Rosner, branch president at Haag am Hausruck, Austria. Brother Rosner looked very thin, but otherwise was in good spirits. He said he had been getting along fine since he was blessed and healed in his home in 1938.

It was on December 6, 1938, that I had had the privilege of visiting Haag am Hausruck with my mission president, M. Douglas Wood, and his wife Evelyn. When we arrived at Brother Rosner's home we found him in bed recovering from a serious accident.

As I recall, he had been working in some kind of cistern when one of its sides collapsed and crushed him in the bottom. When he was removed, more dead than alive, it was determined that his back was broken and his ribs badly crushed. During his most recent visit to the home, the doctor had told Brother Rosner, in effect, "Mr. Rosner, you may live, but you will never live to walk again."

We planned to meet with the saints in meeting that evening. Brother Rosner insisted that he wanted to attend the meeting, saying, "I have faith that if I go I will be made well."

We could not deny his faith. After giving him a blessing, we made a crude "Boy Scout" stretcher, loaded him on it as carefully as we could, and carried him into the meetinghall. One end of the stretcher was resting on a chair so that he could observe all that took place.

Brother Johann Thaller of Munich was the second speaker that evening. He paused in the course of his remarks and, looking down at Brother Rosner, said, "Brother Rosner, I feel that because of your faith you will be made whole." It was an electrifying experience.

As our meeting ended, Brother Rosner declared that he could now walk, but would not do so since he was not wearing his trousers. We carried him into his home. As we entered the kitchen, he got out of the stretcher and walked to his bed unaided.

During the war years, Brother Rosner traveled many times all over Austria on his bicycle in his efforts to keep in touch with the saints and bring help to them when they were in distress.

At the end of our meeting in Vienna, a young man of about nineteen, wearing a shabby army uniform, walked up to me and asked if I remembered him. When he told me his name, I had to confess that it did not ring a bell with me. Did I remember the young boy in Haag am Hausruck whom we had blessed back in 1938 during our visit there? he asked.

When I replied, "Yes," he said, "Well, I'm that young man."

The night after we had blessed Brother Rosner and had witnessed his amazing recovery, I had found it difficult to sleep. My mind continued to marvel at what we had just witnessed.

Early the next morning a young girl, about eight years old, knocked at the door. She asked: "Are you the missionaries?"

After we had responded, she continued, "I have a brother who is very sick. He would like you to come to our home to bless him before you leave. But we're not members of your church."

We gladly went with her. Her mother was a widow living in a limited space on the second floor of one of the village homes. As we entered the home we found a tear-stained mother heating pans of water on her little coal stove. She explained that her son had some kind of disease of the leg that had resulted in poisoning. Since the poison was now reaching the hip, she was waiting for a doctor from a neighboring community to amputate the boy's leg at the hip in order to save his life. The hot water would be needed, since the doctor would have to perform the operation on the kitchen table.

How well I recalled that scene! The little boy—about eleven years old—had a leg so badly swollen he could not wear any trousers. The poison streak was quite visible. He stopped crying, although in great pain, and said, in effect: "I'm not a member of your Church, but I've been going to your Sunday School where our teacher told us that you can bless people and make them as well as Jesus did. I want you to make me well!"

It was a sobering request, but we blessed him that according to his faith he should be spared.

Now, seven years later he stood before me, a priest in our Church, healthy and well. He had served briefly in the German army. Meeting him and Brother Rosner that night was a wonderful climax to a most inspirational meeting with the Viennese saints.

Although Vienna was a so-called "free" city—partitioned in four sectors, as Berlin was—the people were living in constant fear of molestation by Russian soldiers. Vienna, the city of "Gemuetlichkeit," music, and gaiety, gave the appearance of an almost dead city. Everything looked drab and colorless. Apparently nothing had been painted for several years.

This city was badly scarred from bombings and fires. Many Russian soldiers could be seen wandering aimlessly along the streets. People looked gaunt and tired. At that time an International Red Cross bulletin stated:

> Austria [is] one of the countries that has been most grievously affected by the recent conflict...practically no milk or milk products are to be found on the market...Without help from outside, starvation is now practically inevitable...Famine conditions already exist today in Lower Austria, where the population are given rations yielding a maximum of 800 calories a day. According to recent information, rations will shortly be cut down in Vienna owing to the lack of foodstuffs...

At the Dachau concentration camp (near Munich, Germany) we visited the human crematories, and saw the gallows and the trenches in which innocent kneeling victims had been ruthlessly machine-gunned. We saw the kennels in which prisoners had been thrown and then torn to pieces by ferocious dogs which were kept there.

In this camp alone, 238,000 persons were exterminated. Some of the ashes of the victims were sent to their near relatives, who were required to pay a stipulated sum for them or suffer themselves in turn to be subjected to the horrors of such a camp. The posted signs suggested that approximately 20 million persons were thus systematically and brutally killed in this and the other three hundred such camps established by the Nazis.

The examples of fiendish brutality that were here related to us made us sick at heart. Among other "souvenirs" were lamp shades made of human skin and special implements of torture reminiscent of the Inquisition period of the Middle Ages. When we visited Dachau, over twenty-thousand SS troops (Blackshirts) were confined to the prison barracks awaiting trial on charges of war crimes.

President Max Zimmer later told us that plans had been discovered in the German embassy in Switzerland, after cessation of hostilities, for the construction of five such concentration camps in Switzerland by the Nazis after their planned seizure of that nation; that German troops had been at the borders for the intended invasion, but the heavy losses and unexpected reverses at Stalingrad necessitated redeploying the troops at the Swiss border and thus the invasion of that land was averted.

As we entered Stuttgart we were impressed that though the damage was heavy, it did not appear to be as extensive as in several of the larger cities we had visited. Here President Benson delivered a powerful sermon regarding the Church attitude toward laws and governments. "It is only in lands where freedom and liberty are enjoyed," said he, "that we can effectively carry on the Church program. In helping to establish such a government in this land, you are helping to establish the work of God. If this or any other nation desires to be happy and avoid future wars of annihilation, it must accept and administer laws based upon freedom and liberty as endorsed by Jesus Christ in the 101st section of the Doctrine and Covenants."

In this meeting the "K-Ration Quartet" sang "Let the Lower Lights Be Burning," to the delight of the entire audience.

When we arrived at Basel, Switzerland, the following day, President Benson learned of the serious illness of his youngest daughter, Beth. He learned further that during this illness, Presidents George Albert Smith and J. Reuben Clark, Jr., as well as Elder Harold B. Lee, had made several visits to his family and had administered to Beth, petitioning the Lord to spare her life.

President Benson later wrote movingly of this experience, entitling the account "The Power of Prayer." Since it reflects so well his feelings on this occasion, it is best to let this account relate what took place.

> Following our first trip after the Second World War through the occupied areas of Germany and Austria, I arrived in Switzerland. Awaiting me was an urgent letter from my wife, sentairmail nearly two weeks earlier. In it she indicated that our youngest daughter was critically ill and that, as was her practice, she had tried to keep this news from me so as not to hinder me in my work. Having been advised by the attending physicians that her life was in the balance and beyond the efforts of their skill to preserve, she urged me to join my faith and prayers with her own. She had tried unsuccessfully to reach me earlier.
>
> Realizing that at this late date the crisis must have been reached without the benefit of my own faith and prayers, I found myself hoping that the prayers of my loved ones had been equal to the occasion. It struck me forcibly how helpless I was to assist at this late date.
>
> I was scheduled within two hours to be the main speaker at the beautiful new chapel in Basel, Switzerland. Hundreds of people from many parts of Switzerland would be there to learn about our visit just completed.
>
> I was torn with such anxiety that I felt unable to participate unless I could be assured of my child's welfare. Yet to get word at this late hour was a practical impossibility. Previous phone calls to the United States had required one to two days to complete and connections were frequently very poor. I was at a loss to know what to do.
>
> Faced with such a problem I realized I must seek my guidance and assurance through my Heavenly Father. As I prayed at

my bedside in the quiet of my room, I received the overwhelming impression to place a phone call without delay. Much to my joy, and somewhat to my astonishment, the call was completed in less than ten minutes. My wife's voice was as clear as though she were in the room at my side.

What a sense of gratitude and relief I felt to learn that the crisis had just passed! Our beloved baby daughter would live. How sweet to hear my wife reassure me that their faith and prayer had been equal to the trial!

To receive those comforting words so filled my soul with joy and thanksgiving that I shall never forget that memorable Sunday afternoon.

That evening President Benson gave an inspiring sermon, but it carried even greater manifestations of gratitude and appreciation because of this experience. During the course of the meeting a small group of children presented us with lovely bouquets of flowers and then sang in English, "Welcome to All." We were deeply moved by such thoughtful affection and decided to respond by having the K-Ration Quartet sing a number, much to the pleasure of those in attendance. This proved to be our last performance as a singing group.

After the meeting, President Benson mentioned how appreciative he had been for the brief personal letters he received from time to time from President George Albert Smith. Usually President Smith wrote along these lines: "I attended sacrament meeting in our home ward [Yale Ward] this afternoon and was pleased to see Sister Benson and her six lovely children all seated together on the front row. All is well!" President Benson regarded this attribute of genuine love and concern as one of the most endearing marks of greatness of that beloved prophet.

En route to London a few days later we visited some of our Church leaders in Belgium. Although it was evident that this nation had been hard hit by the war, the economy was moving ahead at a furious pace. The government had decided to use some of its American funds to buy goods which the Belgians wanted and which those who had the money to pay for them could purchase. There were goods on display which we could not even get in the United States at that time. Although their machinery had been broken down, the Belgian people were working long hours with hand tools to earn the money to supply their wants. This caused the economy to spurt ahead at an amazing pace and proved the value of a system of incentives and rewards.

The following day, Sunday, we held four meetings with the saints in Amsterdam. I was greatly impressed by the enthusiastic singing of the Dutch saints. I do not believe there was a person in the audience in any one of our meetings who was not singing with all his heart. For this occasion there was a special "Singing Mothers" chorus. And—wonder of wonders!—the singers were all dressed in the traditional black skirts and white blouses, so characteristic of this singing group throughout the world. Nearly all of these skirts and blouses had been received from America in welfare packages. Some were rather ill-fitting—some skirts were wrapped around the wearer for about a time and a half, for example—but the sisters looked lovely to me and sang with as much power and harmony as I had ever heard a group of women sing. It was inspirational.

In a special meeting with President Zappey of this mission, President Benson urged him to find some land on which the Dutch saints might possibly grow some potatoes to take care of some of their own welfare needs. We were reminded that land was at a premium, but President Benson suggested that perhaps permission might be sought to use the land of one of the median strips on the divided highway between Amsterdam and The Hague. Subsequent negotiations on this proved fruitful and our first welfare project in Holland was under way. At the end of the first year the Dutch saints had harvested 66 tons of potatoes— sufficient to care for most of their own needs.

Then an unusual request was made of these people. As they were assembled together in a mission-wide conference at Rotterdam to give thanks for the abundant harvest, their mission president, Cornelius Zappey, said: "Some of the most bitter enemies you people have encountered as a result of this war are the German people. We know what intense feelings of dislike you have for them. But those people are now much worse off than you are and we are asking you to send your entire potato harvest to the German saints. Will you do it?"

They did it.

This was a splendid example of the gospel of Jesus Christ in action. The Dutch saints were the first people in Holland to receive permission from their government to ship foodstuffs out of their country. The ministers of government at first exclaimed that such a request was unheard of. "We ourselves are starving and here you want to send food to our former enemies," was their somewhat natural response. Permission was nevertheless granted.

The following year the Dutch saints raised about 150 tons of potatoes. In addition, they went fishing and caught sufficient herring to fill several barrels. Their response to that success was in effect this: "We enjoyed so much giving the German saints those potatoes last year that we want to send them the entire harvest this year along with the pickled herring!" The government granted this request too.

While in Holland, we visited with a married couple from Rotterdam. They requested President Benson to bless both of them so that they might have children. Although they were both relatively advanced in years and had remained childless through the years, they believed that with the Lord all things are possible. Because of their implicit faith, President Benson gave them a wonderful blessing and the promise that their prayerful desire in this matter would be realized.

In 1947, shortly after this mission ended and while working in the Church offices in Salt Lake City, I was invited by Elder Benson to step into his office for a moment.

"Do you remember that sister and her husband from Rotterdam that we blessed to have children?" he asked.

"Yes," I replied, "I remember the occasion well."

"Well," he continued, "I received a letter from them this morning and they enclosed a picture of their first son."

The eyes of both of us clouded with tears of gratitude for this choice blessing made manifest in the behalf of these faithful saints.

Before leaving Holland to return to London, I spent an entire day at the home of President Schipaanboord in Utrecht. He and members of his family recounted some of the problems they had faced during the war years. They showed me some of the false floors in their home where they had hidden the office typewriters, adding machines, records, and other materials to keep them from being confiscated.

On occasion, German troops had come to search the homes for such materials and for the men they knew to be in hiding to avoid being conscripted for forced labor and similar assignments. More than once the soldiers had fired their revolvers into the floors, scattering their shots around. Several times President Schipaanboord or others had been huddled under these floors with equipment all around them, but never were they hit by the shells. They showed me a number of the holes remaining in the floors as evidence of these harrowing experiences.

Before we left Holland, all mission records were completed and a transfer of accounts was officially prepared and signed by both the incoming and the released mission presidents.

Thus ended our first complete tour of Europe. The demands upon our time had been so exacting that neither of us had found time for personal matters except an occasional brief letter to our loved ones at home. Of this period, President Benson remarked: "We were so busy making history that we just couldn't find the time needed to write about it."

As a result of this trip, the way had been opened for missionaries to be readmitted to several European countries. The full cooperation of civil and military authorities with our Church spiritual and welfare programs had been pledged. Permission had been received for the shipment and distribution of urgently needed welfare supplies to our saints in most of the countries of Europe, and negotiations on other countries looked encouraging. One might have felt like adapting a famous wartime quotation by saying, "Never has so much been accomplished so quickly by so few"—except that we were but instruments and witnesses of the power and purpose of our Lord who is at the helm.

chapter six

The British Move Ahead

Upon our return to our London office, President Benson was greeted by at least a bushel of mail and assorted packages. Among these letters was one from an army doctor with whom he had been in lengthy conversation during our recent trip. It dealt with the serious moral conditions then existing among our occupation troops in the American zone of occupation in Germany.

After President Benson had read it and had a chance to reflect upon its far-reaching implications, he said, in substance: "Brother Babbel, from the facts here presented and those which Chaplain Badger related to us, we will see within twenty or twenty-five years a new generation growing up in our country such as our nation has never known before. They will be a generation void of moral restraints of all kinds, having no respect for law and order, for life or for decency. America will have to pay a terrible price for the indiscretions now being committed and for the disease which is spreading like a scourge. You and I will live to see it."

The following day he sent a copy of the doctor's letter, along with his comments, to the First Presidency so they might in turn be fully aware of these foreboding developments. Then we prepared our itinerary for the balance of April and the months of May and June. It reflected the pace we were maintaining and was typical of our entire time together in Europe. This schedule was as follows:

April 19	To Basel, Switzerland
April 20-21	Swiss Mission Conference
April 22	Return to London office

April 23-26	London office
April 27	To Newcastle-on-Tyne, England
April 28	Newcastle district conference at Sunderland
April 29	Leave Newcastle for Bergen, Norway
April 30-May 7	Tour Norwegian Mission
May 5	Conference in Bergen, Norway
May 7	Conference in Oslo, Norway
May 8	Depart for Gothenburg, Sweden
May 9-13	Tour Swedish Mission
May 14	Leave for Copenhagen, Denmark
May 15-16	Tour Danish Mission
May 17	Leave by plane for Rotterdam, Holland
May 18-19	Rotterdam conference
May 20	To London via plane
May 21-30	International Agricultural Conference
May 31-June 7	London office
June 8-10	British Mission Conference
June 11	To Copenhagen, Denmark, via plane
June 13	To Germany via car
June 14	Meeting with saints in Kiel, Germany
June 15	Meeting with saints in Bremen, Germany
June 16	Meeting with saints in Hamburg, Germany
June 17	Meeting with saints in Hannover, Germany
June 18	To Berlin, Germany
June 19-20	Meetings with saints and military in Berlin
June 21	Leave for Cologne, Germany
June 22-24	Meetings in the Ruhr District, Germany
June 25	Handle welfare matters in Frankfurt, Germany

Then to London via Paris, Brussels or The Hague.

The sheer volume of correspondence represented an almost endless task. At times even working eighteen hours a day seemed futile in relation to the mountain of work. However, I was able to get out as many as 104 letters and reports—some of them from four to ten pages long, single-space typing—in one twenty-five-hour period of typing which lasted from 4 a.m. one day until 5 a.m. the next. This seemed to break the backlog. Yet all we were doing somehow seemed insignificant in comparison with what needed to be done.

During the Easter season, while President Benson was attending a mission-wide conference at Zurich, Switzerland, I attended services at the South London Branch. As I entered the little chapel at Ravenslea, the branch president met me and asked if I would speak during the service.

Right after the administration of the sacrament, the silent movie "King of Kings" was shown while the choir hummed and sang various appropriate songs. After seeing this film, my heart was overflowing with joy and gratitude. I was led to speak of the reality of the resurrection in relationship to the restoration of the gospel in our day through the instrumentality of the Prophet Joseph Smith. I felt the Spirit of the Lord very strongly while speaking.

After the meeting a Sister Downs, a faithful member of forty-six years standing, came and spoke to me. She told me that, during my talk, she had beheld with her spiritual eyes, seeing a beautiful personage just slightly behind and to the right of me. She had removed her glasses, thinking that she was imagining things, but the vision remained the same. Since she was nearly blind without her glasses, she realized that what she saw was not a figment of her imagination. The experience had done much to strengthen her faith, she said.

Without telling him what had happened, I inquired of the branch president concerning this sister. He considered her not only completely rational, but highly spiritual as well. I concluded that she had indeed seen with her spiritual eyes on this occasion and that I had not been mistaken about the strength of the Spirit present.

One day during this period, President and Sister Hugh B. Brown went with us in our car to Birmingham, England, for a special meeting with the district presidents of the British Mission. It was a genuine pleasure for me to enjoy the rich exchange of experiences and observations on the way. I was particularly impressed that President Brown insisted in riding in the less comfortable back seat with Sister Brown, rather than being separated from her. This love and tender concern for his sweetheart and companion magnified President Brown's stature in my eyes and heart.

En route to Birmingham we passed through Coventry. President Brown showed us the ruined cathedral and the other extensive bomb damage. He explained that modern coventry was best known, before the war, as one of the great centers of Britain's automobile and cycle industry. Now it had become a symbol of the 1940-41 "blitz" with which the Germans attempted in vain to crush Britain's population and war production centers.

The famous attack on Coventry did more permanent damage to the beautiful medieval buildings of the city than to the great war plants which lay on its outskirts. The old, half-timbered Tudor houses in the center of the city suffered considerable destruction, and the Cathedral—one of the finest examples of perpendicular architecture in Europe—was left in ruins.

The spirit of Britain, it was explained to us, was shown in Coventry's reaction to the famous bombing attack on November 14, 1940. Of 80,000 persons working there at that time, 77,000 or 96 percent were back at work in fourteen days.

Birmingham is essentially a huge industrial city. It has been said that "Birmingham makes everything from a pin to a steam engine." Throughout the world, in the prewar days, "Birmingham goods" were traditionally the low-price metal goods, hardware, and jewelry that played an important role in British trade. In addition, Birmingham is the center of a vast engineering industry.

In Birmingham lies at the heart of England, only twenty-four miles from the Shakespeare country around Stratford-on-Avon. It is an important center not only of England's intensive railroad system, but also of the highly developed system of inland canals which link the four great ports of London, Liverpool, Hull, and Bristol. When we visited here, its population had risen to over a million, making it Britain's second largest city.

The day following our successful meeting in Birmingham with the district presidents, we arrived in Sunderland. Here President Benson had been the conference president while sewing as a missionary in the early twenties. He was accorded a hearty reception by a host of saints who remembered him from those earlier days.

During the Saturday evening meeting with the saints, President Benson related an inspirational experience in the life of his wife Flora's mother, Sister Amussen. Sister Gladys Quayle, who recorded this account in shorthand, provided me with a copy, as follows:

> This good lady [Sister Amussen] passed away about two and-one-half years ago. We were living in Washington, D.C., at the time. My wife, when she got word, left by plane with my two little girls but did not get to Logan until just a few hours after she passed on, but this interesting thing happened a week before.

> It has probably made a greater impression on the little town of Logan than anything else that has happened there, and assisted the testimony of many people, including several nonmembers.

> On Saturday morning, as I recall, she came into the home of her eldest daughter, who is still living in Logan. This good lady had been living alone—had been a widow for forty years. After going downtown and doing a little work, she came into the home of her eldest daughter and said, "Mabel, the Lord has just made it known to me through my husband that my time has come, that on Thursday it will all be over and I will have passed on."

> You can well imagine what a shock that would be to the daughter, since her mother was apparently in perfect health. She continued: "Your father appeared to me last night—it is not the first time—but he appeared to me last night and told me he had come to tell me my time had arrived, that I should be ready to leave by Thursday of next week, that I should put my affairs in order."

> Then she concluded with, "There is nothing to be excited about. Death is just as natural as birth. I am not worried. I am not concerned. I feel tired."

> The daughter tried to make her believe she was imagining things and her mother replied, "No, I'm not imagining things: It did happen, and what I say is true."

> It did not make a deep impression on the daughter for some

time—at least not enough impression that she notified the other members of the family.

From this place her mother went down, drew out her small savings from the bank, paid her bills, went and selected her own casket and made arrangements for the payment of it, then went back to her home and went on with her usual activities. She did not tell anyone else. Later she even went so far as to call on the electricians to have them come up and turn off the power—the lights—and instructed the plumber to turn off the water. All this happened about Tuesday, as I recollect.

In the meantime Sunday had passed and she had been to Sacrament and fast meeting, and the bishop told me this afterwards: "She bore her testimony, which she usually did on Fast Sunday, but on this particular Sunday she bore her testimony so impressively, it was just like bidding us all goodbye, and she bore it more fervently than I have ever heard her. After she sat down, no one else got up. We just all sat there and finally I got up and announced the closing hymn."

On Tuesday evening she began to feel more or less a weakness and called her daughter and asked if she would send her husband with the car as she would like to spend the next couple of days with her. She even told her daughter which bed she would like to lie down in. She said, "I'll only be here two days and I would like to occupy the room Dick occupies"—(a nephew of whom she was very fond)—and she went to bed and became weaker and weaker.

Her son went in and held her hand and talked a bit, and she told him that by Thursday it would soon be over, and he tried to dissuade her. On Thursday her daughter came to the bedside and for the last time she said, "Mabel, I am going to sleep now. I am weak and tired, but I feel happy in my heart. Don't waken me even though I sleep until the eventide." And she went to sleep and never awakened.

In one of the Sunday sessions President Benson recalled some of the bitter persecutions which were encountered in Sunderland and contrasted those conditions with the present day acceptance of the elders wherever they labor. While I took fairly complete notes of this account at the time, several years later when President Benson was serving as Secretary of Agriculture on President Eisenhower's cabinet, he related this incident in such beautiful terms to a reporter from the *Readers' Digest* that I have included this more complete account here rather than my somewhat limited notes.

Rearing 11 vigorous children to honorable manhood and womanhood on a small farm is no easy accomplishment. Yet, as my father and mother devoted themselves to this task, they never seemed to have any fear of the future. The reason was their faith—their confidence that they could always go to the Lord and He would see them through.

"Remember that whatever you do or wherever you are, you are never alone," was my father's familiar counsel. "Our Heavenly Father is always near. You can reach out and receive His aid through prayer."

All through my life the counsel to depend on prayer has been prized above any other advice I have ever received. It has become an integral part of me, an anchor, a constant source of strength.

Prayer came to my aid during a most terrifying experience of my early life. I was a missionary in (Sunderland) England for the Mormon Church. My companion, William Harris, and I were standing back to back, facing a hostile crowd that was swelled by a rowdy element from the pubs, men who were always eager for excitement and not averse to violence.

What had started out to be a customary street meeting soon took on the proportions of an angry, unmanageable mob. Many false malicious rumors had been spread about our church activities.

The crowd started swaying. Someone in the rear called out, "What's the excitement?" Several voices shouted, "It's them bloody Mormons!" This touched off a clamorous demonstration: "Let's get 'em under our feet!" "Throw 'em in the river!"

The mob surged forward and tried to force us to ground so they might trample us.

In my anxiety, I silently prayed for the Lord's guidance and protection. When it seemed that I could hold out no longer, a husky young stranger pushed through to my side and said in a strong, clear voice: "I believe every word you said tonight. I'm your friend."

As he spoke, a little circle cleared around me. This, to me, was a direct answer to my fervent prayer. The next thing I knew, a sturdy English bobby was convoying us safely through the crowd and back to our lodgings.

Resorting to prayer in such a time of crisis was not born of desperation. It was merely the outgrowth of the cherished custom of family prayer with which I had been surrounded since earliest childhood. How well I remember that while the family was small we frequently knelt together in the kitchen. As we grew in numbers and size we moved into the dining room which had been added. As children we took our turns in offering simple, heartfelt prayers. How grateful I am that we have continued that practice in my own home, and that my devoted wife and children look upon it as a never-failing source of strength and contentment...

It is soul-satisfying to know that God is mindful of us and ready to respond when we place our trust in Him and do that which is right. There is no place for fear among men and women who place their trust in the Almighty, who do not hesitate to humble themselves in seeking divine guidance through prayer. Though persecutions arise, though reverses come, in prayer we can find reassurance, for God will speak peace to the soul. That peace, that spirit of serenity, is a great blessing.

If I could wish for anyone a priceless gift, it would not be wealth, profound wisdom or the honors of men. I would rather pass on the key to inner strength and security which my father gave to me when he advised, "Receive His aid through prayer."[1]

In showing the improvement in attitude, President Benson mentioned a comment by the reporter from the newspaper the *People,* who had interviewed him just before we left for this trip. The reporter said, "This has been the most refreshing hour I have spent in my life. I am grateful to know that there is a people on earth who know where they are going and have such a splendid

---

[1]Excerpts from "The Best Advice I Ever Had," by Ezra Taft Benson, *Reader's Digest,* November 1954. Copyright 1954 by The Reader's Digest Assn., Inc.

program to follow. I would to God that the whole world could know of this program."

As I was driving, in Sunderland, I was reminded of an interesting practice of those days. At night the cars in some of the major cities of Britain would drive with only their parking lights turned on. As cars approached an intersection they would flash on their high-beam headlights. The person whose light first reached the intersection apparently had the right of way. Fortunately, we found the British drivers to be considerate and courteous. During the war they had embedded small saucer-like objects with glass reflectors in the center and along the sides of many streets. The reflection even of the parking lights was sufficient to make night driving a safe and comfortable experience in cities so equipped.

When we left after an early breakfast for Carlisle, the trip took us through the English lake country—probably England's loveliest. We were fascinated to see its breathtaking beauty. Along the way President Benson told us of having gone across this part of the country with President David O. McKay when the latter was serving as European Mission President during the early twenties. He recalled how President McKay would become so enraptured with the beautiful scenery that he would begin to quote Shakespeare, Keats, Shelley, or Burns (or some other great poet), completely forgetting his driving as he looked heavenward. At times he removed his hands from the steering wheel to emphasize certain choice passages of prose with appropriate gestures. More than once, President Benson said, their little flivver would dart off the road and have to be steered back as President McKay would sense what was happening. I was assured that even in those early days the Lord showed his love and care for that great man by preserving his life many times from serious harm or accident.

As we drove, President Benson also told the joke about an American visitor to England who had hired an English guide to show him around. Everywhere they went, the American would make odious comparisons between what he was seeing and something far grander or more magnificent in America.

By the time they finally arrived in this beautiful lake district, the guide's patience had been strained to the limit, but the American did acknowledge that this part of the country was in a class by itself. "However," he added, "if we had this property in America, we'd really make it a showpiece!"

This was the "straw that broke the camel's back." The guide quickly responded: "Well, sir, you could have these lakes in your own country quite easily if you really wanted them."

The American was immediately interested to know how such a thing might be accomplished. His guide retorted: "Well, let me tell you how. All you need is a long piece of pipe. Put one end in our lakes and the other end in America. If you have half as much suck as you have blow, you'll get them there easily!"

All too soon we were in picturesque Carlisle with its famous castle, the one associated with Mary Queen of Scots. After visiting some Church members Elder Benson had known during his earlier mission, we drove to nearby Gretna Green, Scotland, where we visited the famous blacksmith shop, scene of thousands of runaway marriages during the past 150 years. Here couples were married with their hands joined across the blacksmith anvil. Under the laws of Scotland there was not a requirement for either God or the church to enter into the ceremony, so anxious couples (frequently one or both parties being a minor who had been refused parental consent) were united simply by declaring before witnesses their desire to be united in wedlock.

Carved in the wooden walls of this old blacksmith shop were many initials. We were informed that the last official "ceremony" had been performed in 1940. The last official "priest-blacksmith," who served as our guide, assured us that hundreds of thousands of marriages had been performed there through the years. The anvil was supposed to bring good luck, and all wishes made while putting the hands upon the anvil were supposed to be granted.

The following morning we left early for Newcastle and viewed the famous Roman wall, which extends most of the distance between Carlisle and Newcastle. Anciently it was used as a fortification and means of defense against the Scots Most of the way we drove over the ancient Roman road which an its repaired condition, was considered to be a marvel of road construction, although it was nearly fifteen hundred years old.

Newcastle itself is so called because of the "new castle" built there in Norman times, probably upon the site of an ancient Roman fortress. Although this is a heavy industrialized section along the River Tyne, there are still more castles to the mile here than in any other part of Britain. A catalog dating back to 1541 listed no less than 120 castles in a section of this country; and even today there are sixty or seventy remaining. Some are inhabited, but the majority are nothing but ruined shells.

After boarding the S. S. *Jupiter* at Newcastle in a drizzling rain, we watched them store our car in the forward hatch of the ship and then began our trip through a somewhat choppy North Sea. We were advised to expect a rather severe storm en route, which might delay us a day, but the blessings of the Lord, continued with us; we enjoyed the entire trip and arrived on schedule in Norway as we had expected.

chapter seven

Wonderful Scandinavia

As we neared Stavanger, Norway, the sun was shining and we were greeted by the picturesque sight of the broken coastline with its many small islands, each dotted sparsely with white frame houses with red roofs. President and Sister A. Richard Peterson and a number of the local saints were on hand to meet us upon our arrival shortly before 9 p.m.

The story of President Peterson and his missionaries is another example of the Lord's power being manifest in furthering his work. I insert the account here, even though the end of the story took place some time later.

When President Peterson and his missionaries arrived in Norway they were given permission to remain only sixty days. They appealed for extensions. One was granted. Finally they were notified rather forcibly that no further extensions would be granted. Their only recourse was fasting and prayer.

On the very eve of their required departure, the official who had been so adamant and bitter toward them suddenly died of a stroke. When the remaining officials were contacted the following morning, they seemed both willing and anxious to have the missionaries remain indefinitely.

Because the hour was late when we arrived at Stavanger, the ship's captain invited us to spend the night on board ship, which invitation we were happy to accept.

It was still very light. We were informed that in this land of the "midnight sun" there was virtually no darkness at this time of the year (May). A young lady reporter from the largest daily newspaper in Stavanger was on hand to interview President Benson. Two additional interviews were scheduled for the following morning. Excellent publicity resulted from these friendly interviews.

The next morning I ran across the following items in a delightful and descriptive publicity pamphlet about Norway.

Norway is a country fascinating to meteorologists because of its startling and unaccountable weather. For one thing, the fiords, the deep inlets between the mountains, are always free of ice, in spite of temperatures that sometimes get down around fifty below....

Norway is the narrowest country in Europe (about 60 miles wide on the average), the most sparsely populated, the possessor of the most islands, the most mountainous, and the first to give women the vote. It has a hundred and fifty thousand islands, not even counting the little ones, and is three-fifths mountains, which means 73,752 square miles. The coastline, if stretched out straight, would extend from the North Pole to the South Pole...The bottoms of some of the lakes are a thousand feet below sea level.

Perhaps more fascinating than the Norwegians themselves are the lemmings. These creatures belong to the mouse family, but for all that are restless, pugnacious, and fearless. You've heard of their migrations from the mountains to the sea, which are conducted under cover of darkness, the days presumably being passed in sleep. On the march, the lemmings, who are vegetarians, eat the countryside absolutely bare. They are eaten, in turn, by weasels, wolves, and owls, and also by reindeer, who are otherwise vegetarian themselves. When the lemming band, which replaces its casualties with young born en route, reaches the sea, they all jump in and strike out in the direction of England. They are excellent swimmers, but nobody has ever seen a lemming in England....

The Norwegians were the discoverers of the benefits of cod-liver oil. Before the invasion by Germany, the cod-liver oil business was one of the largest in Norway. Another was the export of down from the eider duck. This is so fine that five pounds of it, enough to stuff a whole quilt, can be compressed into a ball the size of a man's fist. Idleness is viewed askance in Norway; the natives boast that the only beggars there are the seagulls. The farmers keep their children tethered like goats, because of the precipices.

One welfare carload of food and one carload of clothing, plus three hundred cases of "Treet" had arrived recently. These supplies were sufficient to meet the pressing needs of our saints in this area.

Brother Gustav Wersland, the branch president, accompanied us on a sight-seeing tour, President Peterson serving as translator. I had never seen any country like this. At one time it must have been nothing but a mass of rocks. Each farmer had removed thousands upon thousands of rocks from his piece of land to render it tillable. Each piece of land I saw had rows upon rows of stones piled one upon another to form miles and miles of stone walls, partitions, etc. For example, many pieces of land about 100 square feet in size had high walls on all four sides—as high as a man could reach—with a small opening to get into the adjoining piece of land. It reminded me of a labyrinth. I felt exhausted just from looking at the hundreds of years of back-breaking labor this must have required to clear the land. It is small wonder that seafood has been the mainstay of the Norwegian diet!

We learned that Brother Wersland had been a leader in the Norwegian underground resistance forces during World War II. As a result of his bravery and exploits he became one of Norway's most decorated heroes and patriots. As he took us past a graveyard of Nazi planes, all pushed together in a large heap during the liberation of Norway, it became evident that he preferred to wipe memories of the Nazis out of his mind.

We were told that on several occasions during the war, German soldiers who were members of the Church attended services, administered to the sacrament, and even administered to the sick. At times they were able to get extra army rations (German) and made these available to some of our saints who were hard pressed for food. Brother Wersland had only the highest praise and admiration for our German LDS servicemen and the love they manifested during the war. We were happy to hear this, because it confirmed what we had been told in the other countries we had visited thus far.

At Brother Wersland's home we learned a few details about the life of this exceptional man during the war years. At one point, President Benson happened to mention the word Nazi. Brother Wersland was noticeably disturbed. Without saying a word, he reached across the table, picked up a milk bottle, and crushed it in his bare hand as if it had been a plastic toy.

Elder Benson and I could scarcely believe what we had just witnessed. President Benson reached over, picked up another milk bottle, and gripped it firmly as Brother Wersland had done. First he pressed it with one hand, then with both, but without success. When he put it down, Brother Wersland picked it up and crushed it as he had the first bottle! In shaking his hand to congratulate him, I discovered that it was covered with a skin as tough as strong leather. He could easily have crushed my hand, had he desired to do so.

We learned that after many harrowing experiences as a leader in the Norwegian underground, Brother Wersland was finally captured and sent to a concentration camp in Germany. He was transferred from one camp to another until he finally found himself in Poland.

Wherever he was sent, he was always under heavy guard. He was threatened repeatedly with extermination. Always he taught the gospel to his captors at every opportunity. Eventually he and sixteen companions were sentenced to die at the hands of a firing squad.

Although his companions were killed, he remained alive. Later, with the help of a German officer who had responded to his gospel message, he was permitted to escape. Eventually he reached Denmark, where he contacted underground workers. With their assistance he was able to return to Norway. Here he took up his duties as a leader in the underground.

Finally his valiant band of men found themselves surrounded by three German divisions. Their ammunition was depleted and their food supplies nearly gone. As far as I was able to piece things together from his account, he prayed to the Lord to know what to do. The next morning he told his men that he was going to drive his motorcycle into the nearest city to seek help and supplies. His comrades considered this to be certain suicide, but his mind was made up. As he rode into the city on his motorcycle he was repeatedly fired upon, but miraculously he escaped injury. In a short while he was among friends.

That night, he and these friends were able to commandeer several German supply trucks loaded with food and ammunition. Then they managed to drive these trucks through the German lines without serious incident. These supplies proved to be adequate to enable them to continue their harassing activities and hold out until their liberation by the American forces.

After visiting with Brother Wersland, we enjoyed an overnight voyage by steamer to Bergen, Norway. Here we found evidence on every hand of the effectiveness of the Church Welfare Program. Most of our members were dressed in American clothes and were looking robust and healthy.

We were taken through the fish market. Most of the fish were swimming in special containers built into the bottom of the fishing boats. Certain varieties could only be sold alive. We watched one family select a nice-looking fish. The lady operating this particular booth reached down with a hand fishnet and brought the desired fish to the surface. Then she placed it on the counter and, while it was still squirming, took it in her hands, covered it with some kind of burlap cloth, and skinned the fish alive while we were standing there. It was still wriggling when she wrapped it in a piece of newspaper for the customer. That fish had to be fresh!

After we had visited two proposed sites for a chapel, President Peterson took us to the top of a steep cliff known as "Fløi Fjellet." From this vantage point he wished to show us the desirability of the chapel sites we had seen—since here we could literally look down upon the entire city, much as we might from a low-flying plane. We reached the top by means of a special cable car that took us up a forty-degree incline. President Peterson told us that President David O. McKay had visited this spot during one of his worldwide tours and had pronounced this the most magnificent view he had ever beheld.

One could see for miles in all directions. Nestled at the base of this cliff was the picturesque city of Bergen with its vari-colored patchwork of parks, lakes, red roofs, and wharves. One could see an entire fiord stretch out into the North Sea. Two other breathtaking fiords could be seen stretching inland for miles. Precipitous mountains and cliffs surrounded us in all directions. Dozens of ships were wending their way in and out of Bergen Fiord, many of them appearing as tiny specks upon the waters stretching far inland. The atmosphere was so clear that we could see for miles into the North Sea, with its myriads of large and small islands nestled along the rugged coastline.

Later in the day I mentioned to one of the members, who spoke fairly good English, what I had read about children being tethered much like goats on the top of the cliffs rising above the fiords. He then told me how in some of the rural sections of northern Norway they still had a unique custom. In the fall of each year the mothers would bring their little children and youngsters together and sew them up in their flannel underwear for the winter. They would not change all winter long, but would permit the body oils to accumulate as a shield against the raw, cold weather. As a result—so I was informed—they were able as a people to avoid almost entirely the common cold, pneumonia, and related illnesses. Then in the spring of the year these mothers would bring their children together again and have a "ripping bee," during which the winter underwear would be removed and the children bathed.

Among others, we met a Brother Art Wilford, who had just recently returned from a long period of convalescence in Sweden. He told a fascinating story of how he had been captured while serving as an underground member in Bergen. Then he was sent to one concentration camp after another in Germany, where he suffered all kinds of indignities and diseases. Finally he managed to escape, more dead than alive, and wound up in Sweden so physically weak that no one expected him to live. After weeks that stretched into months, he finally recovered sufficiently, as a direct result of prayer, to get around on crutches. He was still using these when we met him.

En route from Stavanger to Oslo a few days later we traveled by car, along the way skirting around many fiords which kept us spellbound. One valley in particular was framed by rolling hills covered with the laciest fringe of trees I had ever seen. Below was a silvery mountain stream cascading from rugged heights through the lazy village toward the mouth of the fiord. And beyond the mouth were the shining waters of the ever-changing North Sea. The scene seemed to combine almost every element of beauty imaginable. This spot, known as Kvinnesdahl, is considered to be one of the two most beautiful sights in Norway.

It was fairly late when we arrived at Fevik, at the mouth of another gorgeous fiord. The sun was still shining brightly, so we decided to visit together until the sun went down. Finally at 2 a.m. we watched the sunset and retired to our beds—only to be awakened by the brilliant rising sun just one hour later! We had had a long day, and since I was still tired I pulled the shades down in my room and "slept in" until 5:30 a.m. Shortly thereafter we continued our trip on to Oslo.

This drive took us through beautiful forested country studded with hundreds of lakes and picturesque islands. Much of the highway was being chiseled through stone or granite cliffs. It was astonishing to see that practically every piece of construction was done with hand tools rather than the pneumatic hammers, drills, etc., I was accustomed to seeing in American construction work.

There were seemingly thousands of twists and turns, horseshoe bends, and even corkscrew turns, all of which made for very deliberate driving, but which enabled us to take our time to enjoy the magnificent scenery.

After a series of profitable meetings in Oslo, we left for Sweden. President Benson was driving as we reached the Swedish border. After we had cleared customs, he continued driving on the right-hand side of the road as is the custom in most European countries. Suddenly we were approached by a Swedish driver from the opposite direction, coming straight at us. President Benson was visibly annoyed as he said, "Doesn't he know enough to stay on his side of the road?"

I hurriedly reminded him that in Sweden people drive on

the left-hand side of the road, the same as in Britain. With a hurried smile he quickly swung over to the lefthand side of the road and avoided what might have been a serious accident.

One of the sisters who requested a blessing in Gothenburg was a wheelchair invalid. She appeared to be suffering from acute arthritis. We learned that her parents had objected so strenuously to her joining the Church that, in spite of her nearly helpless physical condition, they had legally disowned her and left her to take care of herself as best she could. The saints had been of great assistance, but she wanted to be of service herself. As she requested President Benson to bless her, she expressed the hope that she might one day preach the gospel to her loved ones and the people of Sweden. President Benson blessed her that, according to her faith, her desires should be realized.

We learned several months later that this sister had been called on a mission. Through her faith she was able to leave her wheelchair and fulfill an outstanding mission. Still later she was able to emigrate to the United States and engage in ordinance work in the Salt Lake Temple.

Two of the local newspapers in Gothenburg carried excellent articles concerning President Benson and his visit. This favorable publicity was a marked change from conditions encountered a few years previously. We were accorded the same considerate treatment by the press in Joenkoeping, Oerebro, Gaevle, Stockholm, Norrkoeping, and Malmö.

Our trip from Joenkoeping to Oerebro took us nearly 135 miles along the shore, of the second largest lake in Sweden. The scenery was magnificent. At Oerebro we were greeted by a picturesque old castle surrounded by an ancient moat—a castle which seemed to be in excellent condition in spite of its age. I was profoundly impressed by the luxuriant beauty of this choice land. Perhaps this is why many of our Scandinavian members have been disappointed by the abundance of barren wastelands in the Intermountain West.

Sweden appeared to have a plentiful food supply. One day, en route between cities, we ate luncheon at a "Consum" or cooperatively operated restaurant. President Benson waxed eloquent in his praise of cooperatives (with which he was associated in the

U.S. for many years) until he saw a woman coming in to eat with a dog under her arm. Then he exclaimed: "It looks as if even the Consums are going to the dogs!"

During our rather brief visit to Gaevle we stopped to see the home where Peter A. Forsgren was living when he was baptized on June 19, 1850, by his brother Elder John E. Forsgren. This was the first baptism in Sweden by divine authority in this dispensation. The house is unpretentious. It is situated on one of the narrow alleys and was, at that time, painted a bright Swedish red.

During our seven-day stay in Sweden we were able to visit seven of the branches in that mission and to participate in twelve meetings with members and friends. In each city we were given an enthusiastic welcome and had the small meetinghalls filled beyond capacity. The prospects for missionary work appeared to be very favorable.

For some time it had become increasingly evident that the weight of President Benson's responsibilities was causing him frequent sleeplessness. Wherever we went, he desired the privacy of a room alone. From my observation he not only talked matters over with the Lord, but the Lord was not unmindful of him and was pleased to reveal to him things beyond the normal comprehension of man. After each such experience he appeared to gain new strength and insight.

From Sweden we went to Denmark.

Although our stay there on this trip was very brief, we were able to attend meetings in Copenhagen, Aarhus, and Aalborg, three of Derunark's chief cities. As we traveled from place to place I was impressed by the flatness of its fertile land. The largest mountain in Denmark, which they call "Heavenly Mountain," is about 560 feet in height. This nation consists of a number of islands, some joined together by bridges and others connected only by ferries. One of the interesting features was the way the cows were pastured. They were staked in long straight rows, each on a rather short rope so that it could eat all the grass within the immediate vicinity and no more. Then it was systematically moved and allowed to eat another swath. This method obviated the need for fences and ensured that no pasture was wasted. Denmark had lost much of her dairy stock during the war but was still a very rich dairy country.

At our meeting in Aalborg, President Benson spoke more powerfully than I had ever heard him speak—just as I imagine one of the great prophets of old might have spoken. I became so entranced that I neglected to take complete notes.

He warned the people that the Lord had decreed wars and desolation among the inhabitants of the world, that peace conferences would fail and that nations would continue to have unrest and strife until the leaders of nations and their peoples repented, humbled themselves before God, and appealed to God in mighty prayer and in faith. He warned that the present so-called peace would only be temporary, that the time would shortly come when men's hearts should fail them, when they should curse God and die, when the scourges and pestilences decreed should be poured upon the wicked without measure. But he added the Lord's words, "It is my purpose to take care of my saints."

Our next stop was Amsterdam. President and Sister Zappey were waiting for us at the airport. Both were pleased to report that, as a result of President Benson's earlier contacts with government officials, they had been able to purchase a new Citroen car for mission use—the same model as ours, but with many refinements and far greater comfort. This was the first new car to be sold in Holland after the war, and President Zappey reported that even the officials were flabbergasted that the mission was able to make such a purchase when many government officials on priority lists were kept waiting.

Our meetings in Holland were most successful and enjoy. able. The spirit of these Dutch saints helped us understand President Zappey's enthusiasm when he fairly shouted, "You can't beat the Dutch!"

At The Hague we had breakfast in the hotel cafe where three different butlers, all in formal attire and swallow tails, waited on our table. All the breakfast they could serve us was one cup of hot water without any milk, cream, or sugar, and a bowl of oatmeal mush without any milk or sugar. We could have had coffee or tea, with which they would have served sugar and milk and a sweet roll, but we couldn't persuade them to give us the milk and sugar with our hot water. When we mentioned milk, eggs, and rolls with butter, they just laughed at us. But they charged a fancy price for the meal just the same, on the basis that three high-priced men had waited on us hand and foot!

After three days of meetings in Holland, we returned to our office in London. Again we were greeted by an unbelievable stack of mail. We had no sooner arrived than President Benson was informed that he was to attend a five o'clock meeting that day with members of the American Delegation to the International Conference of Farm Organizations being held in London for the next ten days.

After this preliminary meeting he was entertained at a sumptuous reception and banquet at the Savoy Hotel, at which time the delegates were presented to the king and queen and other persons of importance in Britain. Ernest Bevin, Secretary of Foreign Affairs, addressed them. Meanwhile I remained in the office trying to restore order out of the chaotic mass of mail needing attention. Before retiring I completed an up-to-the-minute report of our recent activities for the First Presidency and the *Deseret News*.

Between sessions of the international conference, President Benson was able to phone Geneva and arrange for the International Red Cross to process and ship our welfare supplies by way of the port in Bremen, Germany. Meanwhile two shipments were arriving, and he was greatly concerned about their safe transport to our people. Pilfering of railway cars loaded with food was becoming almost a national pastime. Trains were being stopped by foolhardy bands of people who were desperately in need of food. Efforts were being made to keep such news from "leaking out," but our forwarding agents on the Continent assured us that this was so in spite of the most stringent precautions taken. During all of our time in Europe, however, our shipments suffered only minimal losses of food and clothing. They were successful in keeping probably hundreds of people alive through the terrible aftermath of war.

Britain of course had not suffered the starvation that much of continental Europe had, but conditions were still far from good. I remember that when I arrived in England, I was not prepared for the sharp contrast in living conditions between that country and the United States. Rationing was still in force and was quite severe. Each person received 28 coupons (ration tickets) per six months for clothing, etc. It required 35 for a suit or a dress and 20 for a pair of shoes—plus the cost of the item, of course. It was evident that people could buy but little even when items were available.

The quantity of food was sufficient to sustain life reasonably well, but the fare was simple and the diet monotonous. In cafes a person could order almost whatever he wished; although it would be served in small portions, priced high, and almost invariably boiled to pieces (by the standards of my American palate).

A brief extract from a letter I wrote to my wife in the early summer of 1946 will indicate the supply and prices of some "luxury" items.

> On my way back to the office...I passed a fruit and vegetable stand. Now I've seen everything! Peaches were selling for $1.75 each, apricots for $1.30 each, and small finger-sized carrots for 25¢ each.... Fruits and vegetables throughout most of Europe are either impossible to get or are so sky high that one can't afford such luxuries.

Another thing the war had brought to Britain was the line-up or queue for scarce items or hard-to-get services. An extract from another letter home records my reaction at the time.

> Day after day all over the city you see queue after queue. Sometimes people have to wait four or five hours in such a line, only to be disappointed in not receiving what they want. These queues are dreadful. The time that is wasted, if put to good use, could rebuild the entire British Isles within a year at not one penny expense for labor. I wonder when they'll learn that 'time is money.' I rather doubt that the proposed American loan to Great Britain would pay for two weeks of time wasted in queues. It is the biggest waste of time I have ever seen, but the people humbly and submissively wait their turn patiently, some bringing little folding chairs on which to sit while they wait....

For all my American instincts against such waste of time, I had to admit that the practice had some merit. It reflected the British sense of fairness—you took your turn. The alternative would have been a free-for-all, women-and-children-last approach to the problem of shortages.

After the international conference in London had run its course, we returned to Denmark to pick up our car and begin our second extensive tour of Germany. While we were trying to arrange for the necessary military orders and diplomatic clearances (which didn't materialize before we entered Germany) I ran across a delightful descriptive leaflet concerning Denmark that should fire the imagination of any traveler going there on a visit. Some excerpts from this leaflet follow.

> Denmark, the oldest kingdom in the world, is a remarkably pleasant country—about twice the size of New Jersey and inhabited by four million Danes and three million cows. The cows are always respectfully addressed by their names, which are painted over their stalls, and during the winter they are dressed in overcoats and taken out for a stroll once in a while. The output of dairy products, as you may imagine, is enormous.
>
> The Danes also have been careful to address one another respectfully by their last names, but since these are almost invariably Hansen, Petersen, Jensen, and so on, and their given names are invariably Hans, Peter, Jens, etc., further identification was achieved by mentioning a man's profession or trade: Mr. Butcher Hans Hansen, Mr. Barrister Hans Hansen, and so on. One desperate widow went so far, a number of years ago, as to identify her late husband, on his tombstone, as the Hansen who had had a telephone.
>
> The name situation has been slowly improving in recent years, because the government has allowed a man to change his surname by paying four kroner (the krone was then worth about 21 cents). For a bit over thirty-three kroner, he could copyright a name and from then on be the sole user of it, at least in Denmark.
>
> The highest point of land in Denmark (Heavenly Mountain) is five hundred and sixty-four feet. Under the present [then] reconstruction program beer is again running from faucets in automats; the postmen wear cheerful red coats; people have mir-

rors rigged outside their windows so that they can peek up and down the street without being seen; children shake hands with their parents after dinner; nearly everybody rides bicycles; ladies smoke long, black, thin, twisted cigars in public; the most popular potted plant is the cactus (because it goes so well with the modern Scandinavian style of interior decoration); men as well as women are vigorous and skillful knitters; and the coffee is strong, although the beer (so I've been told) is weak.

Practically every Dane meets the King at one tune or another, riding around on a horse, and the King politely says, "Hello."

All these Disney touches notwithstanding, the Danes are an enlightened and progressive people. Consumers' cooperatives started there in the nineteenth century. The Danes buy fifteen times as many books per capita as do the Americans. In Copenhagen there is a humane version of the institution usually called in America the Home for the Aged. The Danes call it Old People's Town. It has modern flats, parks and gardens, a church, a hospital, and a movie theater. The old people are even provided with pocket money and there arc three hundred attendants for fifteen hundred inmates,

There are a lot of fairly outlandish Danes in history and legend—Hamlet, for example, and Canute, the king who bade the tide turn back.... The greatest Danish writer was Hans Christian Andersen. Thorvaldsen is unquestionably one of the world's greatest sculptors, many of his works being in a class by themselves.

The Danes are practically all zealous Lutherans, but they are also creatures of habit. In one village, for instance, it was the custom, nobody knew why, to bow when passing a certain whitewashed wall of the church. Some antiquarian scraped the wall and found a picture of the Madonna which had been covered up four hundred years before.

Danes eat hot oatmeal with chasers of cold milk and the country women wear cloth masks to protect their skin from windburn. In Denmark the bricks float. It's because they are made of a light volcanic clay. The Jonas Bronck for whom the Bronx is named was a Dane.

chapter eight

Rising from the Ashes

President Benson being bothered with a hacking cough, I drove from Esbjerg (Denmark) to the Danish-German border. This part was under British military control. When we arrived at the border check station, they had a large pole barrier stretched across the road.

We went in and presented our credentials to the British soldier in charge, but were informed that, since we had no military orders authorizing our entrance into Germany, we could not be admitted. President Benson explained that we had tried to make contacts both in Copenhagen and Esbjerg, but had not been able to get through. He assured them, however, that we would be able to arrange quickly for the necessary permission once we reached military headquarters in Germany which were connected by telephone or teletype with Berlin.

This is where President Benson's Washington, D. C., experience came in handy. The guard reluctantly consented to let us past the barrier.

Since our time was getting somewhat short, President Benson got behind the wheel. Usually he drove a little faster than I did, and I must say that he was an excellent driver. Just as they were getting ready to raise the barrier across the road, the British officer in charge of the installation arrived. Apparently when he learned what had just taken place, he ordered the boom to be lowered and the guards at the barrier readied their guns for action. President Benson suggested that I go inside to find out what the trouble was. He said he would keep the motor running and urged me to hurry.

When I entered the small office, I was confronted by a very angry British major. He announced that since we were trying to get into Germany illegally, he had no recourse but to lock us up pending a full investigation.

I began to try to reason with him, but the more I said, the angrier he became. Meanwhile I could hear the motor of the car idling outside. I was praying desperately to know what to say or do. Then a sudden inspiration struck me.

I took out a copy of my Army discharge papers, showed them to the major, and asked him how long he had been in the British army. "Six years," was his reply. We then compared notes briefly on our military experiences.

Next I asked him if he happened to be married. He was. Did he have any children? Yes. His wife, who was living in London, had had a baby boy about a month earlier, and he was looking forward to seeing them both during his next leave.

Now I pulled out a picture of my wife and my daughter Bonnie. I explained that I had come to Europe when my daughter was just a few weeks old, that I was here at my own expense in the interests of finding ways to help people stay alive and become rehabilitated. We had made previous trips into Germany, I told him; we knew the regulations as well as the difficulties; and we would contact Dr. Olsen's office in Berlin for the necessary military orders once we reached a military station in Germany from which we could call.

I showed him my passport and military permit and assured him that our present schedule was already set, that letters had been written to secure military orders, and that we would follow through completely as soon as we reached a point where we could make contact with OMGUS in Berlin.

When I finished, the major professed himself convinced. "Well, if you're that kind of people and will do what you say," he said "I'll grant you permission to enter Germany. And I wish you luck with your mission!"

When I got into the car, President Benson's first remark was, "Well, what took you so long?"

Apparently we had already become so accustomed to having the way opened before us quickly that any extra delay seemed inexcusable. My experience with the major was a reminder that it wasn't really that easy. I for one was grateful that the Lord again had manifested his promise in our behalf that "they shall go forth and none shall stay them, for I the Lord have commanded them." How grateful we were for this divine passport!

The German cities near the Danish border seemed nearly intact, though hunger was stalking the streets. Then as we approached and entered Kiel, we saw a city almost completely devastated and people who were facing mass starvation.

While in Esbjerg I had purchased a number of food items to take to a family in Hamburg, but as I entered the home of the Kiel district president, Brother Kurt Mueller, and saw his wife in bed (she had nearly died two days earlier following a period of starvation and a resultant heart attack), I left with them a large slab of bacon, a dozen eggs, cheese, apples, tomatoes, etc., and they were thrilled. They had a little boy six years old and a daughter of thirteen, both of whom were unusually brilliant but were becoming quite frail.

Three days later when we returned to Kiel for a meeting with the saints, Sister Mueller walked three miles with her family to attend the meeting and was expecting to walk home afterwards. Because of her recent illness we insisted on taking her home in the car, at which she was overjoyed.

After a deeply spiritual meeting with the saints in Bremen, I made arrangements with an army mess sergeant for some rations to eat along the way. He had no K-rations, so he fixed me up with four loaves of French bread, canned fruits, juices, tomato juice, raisins, dried apricots, margarine, oranges, peanut butter, and several other items. We subsequently gave nearly all of these items to the saints. Their delight and gratitude at receiving them seemed somehow to compensate for the meals we missed as a consequence.

At the 10 a.m. meeting in Hamburg we were welcomed by 512 joyous people. Almost without exception they looked to be on the verge of complete collapse from starvation. At I the close of this meeting, President Benson asked all children eight years of age or younger to come to the stand so that he could give them some candy bars and chewing gum. Over sixty children came forward, and each one was given a handful of goodies. Many of them, in resuming to their seats, asked, "Mutti, what is this?" Imagine children five and six years old who didn't know what candy and chewing gum was! To the mothers with children we gave each a bar of soap

As President Benson was handing out the beautiful California oranges to the expectant or nursing mothers, nearly all of these women were in tears. As she came forward, one of them noticed a spool of thread and a needle which we had taken out of our briefcase along with the goodies. (We always carried these with us to take care of rips, buttons that needed sewing on, and other similar emergencies.)

This sister approached me and requested that I ask President Benson if she might have the needle and thread instead of an orange because, said she, "I need them very much." I relayed this request to President Benson. With tears in his eyes he handed her this treasure along with the orange.

As she started walking down the aisle toward her seat, one of the sisters near the front—the Relief Society president—reached out her hand, tugged at this sister's dress, and said, in substance, "I hope you will be willing to share this needle and thread with the rest of us. Our need is also great."

(Sister Benson had been sending us gift parcels of food. On occasion, when packages were slightly underweight, she added needles and thread and other small items which were almost impossible to get in some of the areas in which we were traveling. The needle and thread on this occasion were her contribution.)

I didn't think I would ever live to see such simple things, which in America we take so much for granted, assume such great importance!

Although many of those in attendance were thin, weak, and hungry, their clothes threadbare and hanging loosely from their starved bodies, in their eyes shone the light of truth and from their lips came a testimony of faith and devotion. There were no expressions of despondency or bitterness. We sensed love, hope, and gratitude in all hearts there.

One of the thrilling accounts we learned about during this

meeting demonstrated the genuine spirit behind the Church Welfare program. This was recorded in the European Mission History as follows:

> Screaming air raid sirens and unusually active anti-aircraft batteries announced the beginning of the thousand-bomber annihilation raids upon Hamburg, Germany. Before the night had passed, the city was a mass of flames and smoldering wreckage. Among the thousands of casualties resulting from this first concentrated bombing raid were 28 Latter-day Saints listed as dead and a larger number seriously wounded. During the following two weeks, bombers by the hundreds and by the thousands continued to pour their blockbuster bombs upon this once proud and beautiful city.
>
> When the fires finally subsided and the smoke cleared away, Hamburg had been leveled to the ground. Hardly a building was left standing in the entire area. Somewhere in all the debris were thousands of dead and many more thousands of wounded, either receiving emergency treatment underground or in overcrowded hospitals nearby to which they were being evacuated.
>
> Brother Otto Berndt, the district president of the Hamburg District, although he found himself bombed out for the second time, and homeless, called the members of the Church, who could be contacted, to assemble so they might determine their losses and the relief and rehabilitation needs of the saints comprising the five branches in Hamburg.
>
> It was determined that of the 300 members of the St. George Branch, more than 60 had been killed and a large number were receiving medical treatment. The other four branches, although smaller, suffered proportionate losses. Nearly all were homeless and many had lost practically every piece of clothing, all of their provisions, furniture, etc.
>
> It was mutually agreed that insofar as possible, all should share alike in the things which were yet remaining in the possession of the saints. Family after family brought their entire stores of clothing, food, and household supplies and shared them with their brethren and sisters who were destitute. Many items of clothing were impossible to supply from this source, so a relief fund was established to which all contributed according to their abilities to do so, and these funds were made available to the

Relief Society for the purchase of materials with which to patch up and remodel old garments as well as to sew new ones. The needs of all were supplied according to their particular requirements, no charge being made to any of them.

Of the five branch meeting houses in the area, only the Altona Branch chapel remained This hall was used as a temporary barracks for a large number of homeless families and the remainder were housed in the homes of members whose property still permitted occupancy.

Groups of brethren were sent out and made purchases of small plots of land in the suburbs upon which they built temporary homes for the members, using what materials could be salvaged from the blasted ruins. In a remarkably short time the mammoth job of relief and rehabilitation had been accomplished through the application of basic Church welfare principles with which most of these members were quite unfamiliar, but they had responded unselfishly as true brothers and sisters in the spirit of love and consideration for others.[1]

At Hannover the following day we met with over two hundred friends and members. There were no electric lights (the place having been severely damaged by bombings). There were no window panes. In their place was black cloth or heavy construction paper. When it began raining outside the windows had to be shut, and it reminded us of an earlier meeting we had held there under similar circumstances. President Benson used Doctrine and Covenants Section 134 as his text. It was a timely message and well received.

Before leaving Hannover, Germany, we had large "USA" letters painted in several places on our car in preparation for going to Berlin via the Russian corridor the next day. On this trip we were unaccompanied by servicemen.

When we reached the Russian checkpoint, the Russian officer in charge examined our credentials, inspected our khaki-colored car with its peculiar markings, and became suspicious of us. Then he gave an order of some sort and two of the Russian soldiers removed their pistols from their holster, and pointed them at us.

---

[1]European Mission History, pp. 36-37.

President Benson did not act in the least disturbed, but said to me, "Just keep smiling, Brother Babbel!"

I smiled as best a man could under such circumstances and I must say that I had absolutely no fear since I was with an apostle of the Lord. In a few moments, which seemed much longer, the Russian officer grinned back at us, said "Dobra" (or something that sounded like that), and we were again on our way.

> In Berlin we received details concerning the recent mission-wide conference held in the city of Leipzig from June 5th to 12th…. The Russian authorities permitted extensive advertising. The radio carried announcements three times each day for two weeks in advance, posters were on every billboard in the city and in every streetcar, so that by the time the conference began, nearly every person in the area knew of it. It might also be of interest to add that railroad officials scheduled two special trains which went from city to city to pick up our members and take them to this great conference.

> …A total attendance of 11,981 participated. The Sunday evening meeting alone was attended by 2,082 persons—by far the greatest attendance ever (to this time) to be present at a meeting of the Latter-day Saints in Europe. At a special concert, featuring a mission-wide chorus of 250 voices and an orchestra of 85 pieces, which was held on Monday afternoon, 1,021 were in attendance, and at the Green and Gold Ball that evening 1,261 participated. The beautiful congress hall at the Leipzig zoo, which is being rebuilt, afforded excellent accommodations and hundreds of people became sincerely interested in the program of the church…

> …Events such as these testify stronger than words of the faith and devotion of our saints in these war-devastated areas. This has been without a doubt one of the outstanding events ever to take place among our people in this land. The spirit of faith and courage it has engendered will do much to strengthen them during this very critical period which they now face.

> One hundred and forty saints from the Berlin area attended this great gathering and it was a joy to see and hear their enthusiasm and praise at a meeting held with the Berlin saints Wednesday evening, June 19th.[2]

---

[2]*Ibid.*, p. 32.

In Berlin, 460 saints were present at a meetinghall which was much better than the last one in which we met. This hall had been repaired by the Americans and was comfortable. A wonderful spirit was present.

Here again, as was the case earlier in Hannover, we were greeted by about twenty small children, standing on chairs lining the center aisle. Each had a large assortment of beautiful flowers in their arms. These they dropped in front of President Benson and the rest of us on our way to the stand, creating a most beautiful and profuse carpet of living flowers. By the time we were seated, tears were streaming down our cheeks and we were so choked with emotion that all of us found it difficult to speak.

I recorded the following for the European Mission History:

> Very favorable progress was made in conferences held with leading military and governmental authorities in Bremen, Hannover, and in Berlin. Assurance of continued cooperation has been received and many problems relating to relief, rehabilitation, securing of meeting places, purchase of property, publications, traveling into Poland, communications, prisoners of war, enlarging of our youth program, and other related items were discussed.
>
> Although many difficulties were constantly arising, we are overjoyed with the splendid cooperation we have received and with the soul-stirring faith and courage of our saints wherever we have met them. We feel to thank God for the privilege that is ours of meeting with these devoted saints and of seeing the beauty and strength of the gospel in the lives of our people in this part of the Church.

At a meeting with the district presidents and missionaries, one of the brethren related the following incident:

Three of these brethren were hoarding a cattle or freight car for passage to Berlin for this meeting. Passenger cars were almost non-existent at that time. When the cars were loaded with human passengers, the remainder had to cling to the sides or climb on top. Apparently these three brethren had crawled to the top of one of the boxcars, which was already overcrowded.

In the process of trying to make room, one of the brethren

was knocked off the top and fell on the station platform in front of a steel-wheeled truck that was passing by. Before he could scramble to his feet and move out of the way, one of his hands and wrists was badly crushed.

As he screamed for help, his companions climbed down, picked him up, and set about inquiring where they might find an army field hospital to get medical attention. But the injured brother said, in effect: "Brethren I've come here to go to our meeting in Berlin and I want you to bless me so that I can go."

His companions laid their hands upon his head and gave him a blessing. When they removed their hands from his head, his hand and wrist were made whole and he climbed back on the box-car to continue his trip to Berlin. A few hours later they expressed their gratitude in our meeting for this wonderful blessing.

When President Benson and I left Berlin and returned to the British Zone of Occupation, we tried to find suitable billets for an overnight stay in Bielefeld. None were available because of the forty thousand refugees who had just arrived from the territories now turned over to Poland. We were directed to make inquiries in the city of Detmond, about twenty miles south. Here we were successful. We spent a quiet night there after an inspirational meeting with the Bielefeld saints, where the floral decorations were the loveliest we had seen in our travels to date.

Along the way to attend the Ruhr district conference at Herne the next morning, we passed through the silent ruins of the great cities and industries in the Ruhr valley. Some of the British military officials with whom we had been in contact estimated that the bomb damage inflicted upon one major city, such as Dortmund, Essen, or Cologne, far exceeded the total bomb damage inflicted upon the entire British Isles during the course of the war Multiply this by 100 and you get approximately the bomb damage heaped upon the British zone of Germany alone. The other four zones (which would include those territories which had now been turned over to Poland) also suffered damage as severely as this area, if not more so.

The destruction was simply appalling. I always felt an overwhelming sadness whenever I saw it and thought of the ragged children and innocent people who had been called upon to suffer such extreme physical, mental, and spiritual hardships and injustices. How I longed for the day when we may enthrone righteousness in our lives as nations and overcome war with peace!

In the Sunday morning session of our conference at Herne, the finest spirit we had ever enjoyed was richly manifest. While a children's chorus was singing, President Benson looked at them several times with a most intense expression on his face.

No sooner had the children finished their singing than we heard the Salt Lake Tabernacle choir and organ burst forth in all their glory. Without our knowledge, some of the brethren had concealed radio speakers in the chandeliers. They had tuned in the weekly rebroadcast of this program over Radio Stuttgart, where Captain Fred G. Taylor, one of our fine servicemen, was in charge. Since he was a former missionary in Germany and had an excellent command of the language, he relayed Elder Richard L. Evan's sermonette to us in German.

Many were weeping for joy as the music and singing proceeded This signified Zion and all that it meant to Latter-day Saints. The spirit on this occasion was tender and sweet, yet overpowering in its impact.

When this music ended, President Benson took me by the arm and led me to the pulpit so that I might serve as his translator. He said, in effect: "I hope you were listening carefully as the children were singing. Let me assure you that *they were not singing alone. The angels were singing with them. And if the Lord would touch your spiritual eyes and understanding, you would see that many of your loved ones, whom you have lost during the war, are assembled with us today.)"*

Such a profound impact did this incident have upon me that I wrote to my wife about it a few days later as follows:

> ...President Benson added, "I have never felt the Spirit of the Lord stronger than I do this morning.... The veil between us and the world of spirits is very thin. I feel most strongly that there are others here besides those we can see-some of your loved ones are

here, also some of the leaders of the Church who have passed on. They loved no people more than you who are here. Those in authority in the heavens above are pleased and willing that the spirits of our loved ones should be near us.

"As the children's chorus sang, I looked over toward them several times, for I heard more voices singing than those who are in the group. In truth their voices were mingled with voices from heaven. We have truly had a taste of heaven today."

There was much more said, but it was one of the sweetest, most inspirational times I have yet experienced. Just to think of it fills my heart with gratitude and praise and my soul with humility and love for the blessed assurance that is ours through the message of the gospel…

The following day we were in Langen (near Frankfurt) where we met with 120 refugee saints who had come from the sections now under Polish control. Here a branch of the Church had been organized where there had been no members earlier. In the official European Mission History we included the following:

It was an inspiration to see these poor creatures sit with upturned faces literally drinking in every word we uttered. It was a joy to hear them sing the songs of Zion and to feel of their warmth of spirits and their deep abiding faith in the gospel. After a meeting of an hour and a half, which was altogether too short for them, we mingled among them and took a picture of the group. During our associations not one word of criticism or bitterness was spoken by any member of the group, although they have lost all of their earthly possessions and some of them their entire family.

The saddest moment came later when, with President Zimmer and the local branch president, we drove out to the rough barracks where these people are living. There in the rudest of shelters, without any sanitary facilities whatsoever, we saw from one to four families living in a single room.

The first place we visited had four families living in a single room (22 people), where they slept, ate, and lived. Two-decker bunkbeds were built along the walls on three sides to accommodate the group for sleeping. A small stove in the middle of the rough board floor provided the only heat for the room and for the cooking

Beds were made at night on the floor for the younger members. The occupants range from babies in arms to one lady past 80 years and there were several young people in their middle teens.

These are all persecuted people from Eastern Germany, which is now Poland. They are unwanted in their former homeland and they have come to the American Zone seeking refuge, although technically their coming is illegal since refugees from Poland are supposed to go into the British Zone and those from Czechoslovakia into the American Zone. We were happy, however, to receive permission yesterday for them to remain inasmuch as they have planted gardens and have shown a real desire to help themselves.

There was a fine spirit among them. It was a thrill to hear one of the members of this particular group of 22 tell about them all kneeling in prayer night and morning together in their rough quarters.

Before leaving, we gave them some provisions which we had been able to get together through the generosity of some of our fine servicemen...and have since made arrangements for additional shipments, which are now under way. Permission was also secured to ship in some barracks which we purchased in Switzerland....[3]

While in Frankfurt we held an evening meeting with our saints beginning at 6:30 p.m. Because I was unable to get President Max Zimmer and Brother Ludwig Weiss (district president from Nuremberg) to leave the mission home until 6:45 p.m., President Benson had to conduct the meeting, direct the congregational singing, etc. No sooner had he completed speaking to those assembled than he had to leave with President Zimmer to keep an appointment with the U. S. military officers in charge of Religious Affairs. They left me in charge for the balance of the meeting.

I was led by the Spirit to speak out boldly and strongly against those individuals (members of the Church) who were working underhandedly against Presidents Benson and Zimmer and causing difficulties which could easily lead to the Church being brought into disrepute and to the terminating of many of the fine things being undertaken for our saints. These particular members were those who, for the most part, were either active in

[3]*Ibid.*, pp. 40-41.

the Nazi regime or very sympathetic toward its aims. They were being hunted down by the denazification units. For their own protection they were seeking mission leadership who would not only sympathize with them but would hide them under the guise of their being missionaries or Church workers.

It surprised me that I spoke on these matters without previous thought or contemplation. Many in the audience felt that the message was surely needed.

Driving from Frankfurt to Basel (Switzerland) the next day, we were struck by the almost complete absence of cows, horses, goats, etc., which used to be in that land in rich abundance. We were informed that thousands upon thousands of these animals had been killed in air raids, while others had been slaughtered for food.

Upon our arrival in Basel we were greeted by President Scott L. Taggart, the new Swiss-Austrian mission president, and his three children. (Sister Taggart was confined at the Basel hospital.) President Benson asked me to get the mission records and accounts in shape for effecting an official transfer of responsibilities to President Taggart.

Here we learned that President and Sister Wallace F. Toronto had left the Salt Lake City mission home for Prague, Czechoslovakia, where he would preside over that mission as he did before the outbreak of war.

As a result of conferences at Geneva with officials of the International Red Cross, it was decided that for the present all relief shipments for Germany and Austria would be consigned to President Benson for arrival at Geneva. It was considered that the risk of losses was too great to continue sending them through some of the German and Belgian ports. For the time being President Benson would designate the distribution to be made as shipments arrived in Geneva.

I was directed to return to Germany to continue to work upon mission matters there and then return to London with the car, visiting our Belgian saints en route.

At the German-Swiss border I kidded with the customs officials and was able to get a large load of envelopes and stationery, as well as a tire and tube for the mission car in Frankfurt, into Germany free of duty. President Zimmer was surprised "You seemed to handle that rather easily with the Swiss officials," he remarked, "but just wait until you have to deal with the French officials when we enter their zone."

I decided I would try to handle those officials in much the same way, bringing up irrelevant subjects whenever they mentioned customs. The result was that we were cleared without even having them stamp our passports or look at our baggage. President Zimmer was even more surprised than I was.

When we reached the autobahn (super-highway) President Zimmer expressed the desire to drive the car. I gathered from previous conversations with him that, although he was not an expert, he had done some driving. How wrong I was!

I showed him how to start and stop the car Then I explained the theory of driving, shifting gears, keeping your eye on the road, etc. Since the autobahn has no counter traffic and is wide, nothing could happen—or so I thought.

What an experience! When he took over, he finally shifted into low gear after killing the motor several times. Then he depressed the throttle to the floorboard. I had to watch carefully to keep him on the road. Finally I got him shifted into second gear and again he pushed the throttle to the floor. After several anxious moments I was able to get him to shift into high gear. This accomplished, he drove as though his very life depended upon speed. I didn't know that the car would go 100 miles an hour—we generally drove not exceeding 50—but he literally froze to the wheel and had that car going at the speed of 100 before I could forcibly remove his foot from the throttle and get him to slow down.

I cautioned him to drive more slowly—the speed limit was 50 miles an hour, and besides that he was weaving all over the road—but every time his foot hit the accelerator he refused to take it off until we were practically flying.

Soon, we noticed a convoy of army vehicles in the distance. Rather than slowing down, he floored the gas pedal even harder. Twice I had to rudely grab the wheel, forcibly kick his foot off the accelerator, and apply the brake pedal with all possible force to avert certain disaster.

After we reached a section where we could pull off to the side of the highway, I took over. He watched me and asked again to have another try at it to show me what he had learned. His second attempt was even worse than his first. I have never had a more harrowing driving experience!

En route to Liege, Belgium, the following day I passed through many cities which had suffered tremendous destruction by the heavy air bombardments and also by the intensive shelling of the heavy artillery as it blasted its way through. Cologne was in terrible shape. Durren, a city which had had 350,000 inhabitants, was now a ghost city in which I could not observe a single wall left standing. Probably this destruction had resulted from the Battle of the Bulge. Aachen was equally demolished. The roads were so badly damaged in many places that they were nearly impassable by car. Man's inhumanity to man was a most appalling thing to behold.

As I reached Liege I learned that the Catholics were celebrating their famous "Love of Christ" festival, which takes place once each century. Flags were flying, streets were blocked by long processions of people, and many of our saints were unable to get through to attend our scheduled meeting. It was with great difficulty that I finally managed to get there myself.

This celebration lasts through four weeks. I arrived during the third week. Never have I seen so much ceremony, so many Catholic priests, bishops, genuflections, costly garments, etc. Incidentally, this came on the eve of America's first Bikini atomic bomb test. Mission President Devignez reported that many people in Belgium were afraid that this test would result in a chain reaction that would entirely destroy the world, but I retired without fear and slept soundly.

chapter nine

"The Morning Breaks"

When I left Switzerland to return to London, President Benson decided to visit with President Toronto in Prague, Czechoslovakia, and help him get under way with his duties there. President Toronto had secured plane reservations for Elder Benson to return to London the following Monday evening, but since he had completed his work in Prague and had much pressing business to attend to in London, President Benson decided to try to leave on Sunday afternoon.

The British airline officials (representing the only airline flying from Prague to London at that time) advised him that this was impossible since they already had more passengers scheduled for the flight than they were permitted to carry. When President Benson stressed the urgency of his request, the official in charge responded, "Mr. Benson, if you were the king of England I couldn't put you on that plane this afternoon!"

President Benson replied, "I'm not the king of England, but I still must get to London tonight." (Since the British highly respected their king, there seemed to be no possible way to board that flight.)

After the plane was fully loaded and was preparing to taxi down the runway, the British official noticed that President Benson was still waiting.

"Why are you still waiting? I told you that you couldn't go," said the official.

"I still must get to London tonight," was the reply.

With a strange look in his eye, the official picked up his

microphone and said, "Take two bags of mail off the plane and put Mr. Benson on."

At this, two bags of diplomatic mail were removed and President Benson boarded the plane. Once again the Lord had fulfilled his promise that "none shall stay them."

While Elder Benson was in Prague, he dedicated the monument erected by the saints in 1945 to commemorate the spot where President John A. Widtsoe had stood when he dedicated that land on July 24, 1929, for the preaching of the gospel.

Not long after this, President Alma Sonne, who succeeded Elder Benson as European Mission President, arranged for a series of meetings with the saints in Czechoslovakia. The leaders in our second largest branch, Brno, urged that he plan to meet with them.

When he asked where they planned to hold their meeting, they said they had rented the opera house, which had a seating capacity of sixteen hundred. This astounded President Sonne, since the branch had only approximately thirty members, including the children. When he suggested that they arrange for something more modest, they insisted on the original arrangement.

A few days later when he arrived in Brno and entered the opera house to attend the meeting, President Sonne was overwhelmed to find nearly two thousand people in attendance. They were seated on all the steps and crowded into the corners and in the entrance ways. When he concluded his message, another unsuspected surprise awaited him. The entire audience arose to their feet and gave him a standing ovation that continued for several minutes.

During this period we received a visit from Dr. LeRoy F. Cowles, President-Emeritus of the University of Utah. Later he went with us to the South London Branch, where he spoke in sacrament meeting on how best to develop the spiritual and temporal sides of man. He commented that in some indescribable way we all radiate a spirit of good or evil, weakness or strength, among all we meet. He counseled that we should always pray for the ability and strength to uplift others. He testified that in all of his years at the University of Utah as a member of the faculty and later as president, after making all possible effort, investigation and consultation he always used prayer as the medium through which to solve all his problems. Never once during all those years, he concluded, did he fail to receive the needed assistance through prayer.

President Benson followed by speaking of the home. "Home," he said, "must have love, devotion, humility, gratitude, and the spirit of service, the spirit of confidence, the spirit of worship. This spirit cannot be purchased, no matter how rich one may become. It must be gained through living righteously. That home which has the feeling of being approved of the Lord is a truly rich home, regardless of how humble or lacking in the refinements of outer appearance it may be."

This kind of comment never failed to strike a chord of deep gratitude within me. To my sweet wife back home I wrote:

> ...We don't have a car, nor a home, nor hardly a blessed thing except the very things that make our lives the finest in the world—each other and a precious bundle from heaven. Strange, isn't it, that the things we love most dearly and prize most highly, the things that are eternal both in nature and enjoyment, are the things money can't buy, things which cannot actually be possessed, but can be enjoyed, loved and cherished. Yes, it's a great world....

My personal world had been made greater by my close association with a great man. One of the most thrilling moments of my life was the day I received my official call to this mission. Words cannot express my feelings as I put the phone down after that call from Elder Benson Called to serve an apostle of the Lord Jesus Christ! That initial feeling of the joy and wonder of it all had persisted as I had come to know Elder Benson through months of intimate association I frequently expressed this thought in my letters home, in words like the following:

> I must repeat again and again that the Lord knew what he was doing when he sent President Benson over here. He is a living apostle of God in every way.... I continue to marvel at his unwavering faith, his unflinching courage, his resolute determi-

nation and undaunted spirit.... He not only speaks to God, but he listens, and I'm sure God speaks with him even as he did with his apostles of old. He is a truly great servant of God—one of the humblest, most devoted men I have ever known, so kind in spirit and manner, so without guile, a man surpassing all men I have known...in his deep heartfelt love for the saints of God. It is a real inspiration just to be around him and see how he works.

Daily we continued to feel deep concern for many of our members throughout Europe. The situation in Germany and Austria, to say nothing of our saints in Poland, seemed to be reaching crisis proportions. Hardly a day passed without the receipt of letters and reports indicating mass deaths through starvation, disease and persecutions. Immorality and rape, which had become commonplace in Europe, were now being inflicted upon young girls not yet in their adolescence. The horrible spread of venereal diseases, especially syphilis, even among small children and adolescents, was reaching epidemic proportions. The homeless, the orphaned, and the abandoned children were undergoing indescribable hardships. The infant mortality rate, even among our members, was a matter of grave concern. And yet proposals had been made for further cuts in rations in those nations suffering most severely.

Bulletins from the International Red Cross indicated that the refugees from Poland had been forced to subsist during the previous two months on bread and water, and that bread was becoming less available. There were many casualties en route, and many of the refugees would probably die before reaching their new living space in Western Germany, since all Germans were being required to leave the areas turned over to Czechoslovakia and Poland To make matters even worse, the prospects of only a meager harvest were the subject of almost daily newspaper reports.

All of these situations make us realize even more how important it was that we seek to establish the kingdom of God and his righteousness in order to generate the divine power to moderate these conditions and open new avenues to solutions.

During this period, Finland was dedicated for the preaching

of the gospel. Since I did not accompany President Benson on this trip, I include the following account from the official European Mission History.

Nearly all of our members in Finland live in Obo and one member in Helsinki (Helsingfors). In checking the records of the branch at Larsmo, President Benson learned that for ten yours they have had a 100 percent record of attendance at all meetings, in their observance of the Word of Wisdom, and in their payment of tithes and offerings. Such a record seemed incredible.

When he questioned them that this was most unlikely because of illness and other problems, they answered, in effect, "Yes, sometimes they do get sick, but we bring them to meetings just the same because this is where the Lord wants them." This wonderful attitude surely confirms President Benson's inspiration in sending missionaries here to open up this choice land.

On Monday, July 15th, President Benson was joined by a sizeable group of members and the missionaries working there. Together they traveled by motor boat to a small island called Lovskar, where during the summer months people cooperatively take their cattle for grazing. Usually they go to the island toward evening, milk their cows, stay overnight on the island in small cabins provided for this purpose, milk their cows again the following morning, and then return to the mainland.

In one of these cottages, owned by one of our members, a small meeting was held during which the history of the missionary work in Finland was discussed and extracts read from the history showing only sporadic missionary work among the Swedish-speaking population of that land since 1861.

Upon learning that none of the General Authorities of the Church had ever (apparently) visited this land, it was decided to locate a suitable spot from which this land might be dedicated to the preaching of the restored gospel. Such a spot was selected on an elevated rise about one-half mile south of the Grev School, bordering near the Larsmo-Jakobstad highway.

Early in the morning on Tuesday, July 16th, President Benson and party, accompanied by a group of 16 saints, visited the spot and conducted dedicatory services. The service commenced with the group singing, "The Spirit of God Like a Fire is Burning."

Elder C. Fritz Johansson offered the invocation, following which President Blomquist briefly reviewed the history of the missionaries who have labored here since 1861, relating their successes as well as their persecutions.

Then the country of Finland was dedicated for the preaching of the gospel. Elder Ezra Taft Benson of the Council of the Twelve, now serving as President of the European Mission, offered the dedicatory prayer.

The morning was beautiful, the sun was shining, the birds were singing, and the prayer offered was so inspirational that those present could feel that the angels and those who had passed on to the spirit world from this goodly land were rejoicing on this memorable occasion. Tears of gratitude expressed the feelings of all those present—an event they shall never forget. It was suggested that the spot be marked in order that at some future time a small monument to commemorate this event might be placed here....

Wednesday morning at 4 a.m., July 17th, the party left for the capital city of Helsinki (Helsingfors) to the tune of "America" and "God Be With You Till We Meet Again," both sung in English by the Larsmo branch choir, who had assembled for this occasion.

They were met later that day in the capital city by our one member of that city, Brother Urho Karppa. He accompanied them to the Helsinki Hotel where they were enthusiastically welcomed by Juho Himalainen, president of the Finnish-American Club, and a group of press reporters and photographers who expressed the hope of their fellow citizens that full-scale missionary work in this land be undertaken. In all of their reports they were most generous and favorable.

At the public meeting held in the Balders Hall—centrally located near the great market place—245 were in attendance and showed an unusually great religious interest and receptiveness to the gospel message, which was most encouraging. They listened eagerly to the account of the restoration of the gospel and after the meeting purchased all available literature and asked for more. Among those present were several of their prominent citizens.

This service was conducted in English and Swedish. It was learned that one large delegation in attendance remained throughout the service even though they could not understand a single word of *either* language used. They expressed the hope that it would be their pleasure to attend another meeting soon conducted in Finnish that they might understand the proceedings and more fully enjoy the spirit which they felt.

Following the meeting, President Benson was interviewed by Finland's national agricultural publication staff...[1]

This public meeting in Helsinki came as a great surprise. Our only member there, Brother Urho Karppa, a convert of about eight months, had written us in London requesting permission to hold a meeting with President Benson during his visit there. We assumed that because of his newness in the Church he did not understand that he was welcome to meet with President Benson at the Helsinki Hotel, since he insisted that he was securing space at Balders Hall.

When President Benson and his party were greeted by an audience of 245, some of whom could not understand either Swedish or English in which the meeting was conducted, it might well go down in history as one of the greatest one-man proselyting jobs in the history of the European Mission.

At the urgent request of some of the Finnish leaders, President Benson wrote the following letter to U.S. President Harry S. Truman upon his return to London:

Dear Mr. President:

Since early February I have been representing my Church on a religious and relief mission in the various countries of Europe. I have just returned from my first visit to Finland, where I held a number of well-attended public meetings in the principal cities. Everywhere I was received with the utmost kindness. Never at any time or in any other place have I heard so much favorable comment regarding the United States.

At the urgent request of some of the Finnish leaders, I promised to write you and express to you on behalf of the Finnish people their deep gratitude to the American people and their leaders for the unselfish assistance which the nation has rendered to the Finnish people through the years. I am free to admit that these sober-minded, solid, splendid people completely won my heart.

[1]European Mission History, pp. 89-92.

I have noted during my absence from my home in the States many perplexing problems which confront you. May a kind Providence endow you with wisdom and inspiration in carrying the great responsibilities of your all-important office.

Faithfully yours,

Ezra Taft Benson

The following spring (after completing his mission to Europe) Elder and Sister Benson were on the train from Salt Lake City to the East on official Church business. One matter which weighed heavily on Elder Benson's heart was that of finding a worthy Finnish-speaking Church member to serve as mission president in Finland.

When the train stopped briefly in Kansas City to discharge and pick up passengers, Elder and Sister Benson hurried over to an adjoining passenger island to buy a late edition newspaper. Although the conductor had announced a ten minute stop, the train pulled out within five minutes and left Brother and Sister Benson behind.

Elder Benson quickly phoned the airport and made immediate plane reservations from Kansas City to Chicago. He then phoned President John K. Edmunds of the Chicago Stake to have someone meet them in a car at the airport so that they could arrive at the railway station in time to board their train for their continuing journey.

Elder Henry A. Matis, President Edmunds' counselor, met them at the airport. As they were speeding toward the railway station, Elder Matis inquired anxiously about conditions in Finland. He was concerned for the safety of some of his relatives living there. This led Elder Benson to inquire about his ancestry He learned that Elder Matis was a convert born of Finnish parentage and that he spoke the language with some fluency. This was the man for whom he had been searching! When Elder Benson reported his findings to the First Presidency, they concurred and appointed Elder Matis to preside over the Finnish Mission, an assignment he fulfilled with distinction for seven years.

Thus a promise that Elder Benson had made to a group of leading business men in Helsinki that "the gospel shall soon be preached in this choice land [Finland] in your own native tongue" was literally fulfilled!

There is another inspiring sequel. Finland became the first country in Europe to have its genealogical records completely microfilmed for the Church Genealogical Society. This was possible through the efficient record-keeping of the Finnish Lutheran Church. President Matis was instrumental in consummating these arrangements. Later he learned that he was a descendant of Bishop Isaac Rothovius, the prominent early Lutheran Church leader who had initiated the record-keeping system for Finland.

Finland is now a flourishing mission rivaling its Scandinavian neighbors. It is also a witness of the inspiration of President George Albert Smith wherein he promised President Benson in his setting apart that he would be instrumental in opening the gospel in new lands. Truly, "The Morning Breaks, the Shadows Flee..."

chapter ten

Caught in a Vortex

After World War II, large sections of land, which had comprised much of Eastern Germany before the war, were turned over to Russia and Poland. To lessen future difficulties with minority groups, the approximately 15 million Germans living in these areas were required to leave and resettle primarily in the new nation of West Germany.

Due to the scarcity of food, clothing, transportation, and funds, the plight of these displaced and homeless refugees was one of the most serious problems faced in the aftermath of the war. To make matters worse, the prevalent spirit of revenge and retaliation had prevented many of these people from leaving during the first few months following the end of hostilities.

Among those remaining behind were scattered groups of our saints in the territory acquired by Poland. What information we could gain confirmed the fact that their plight was desperate and that the lives of many of them literally hung in the balance. We had no time to lose in somehow reaching and assisting them just to stay alive while we worked out the means for helping them with the bewildering task of resettlement and rehabilitation. It was extremely urgent that we go to Poland and get this work started.

Since we would have to enter Poland by way of the air corridor which the Russians had established between Berlin and Warsaw, it was necessary for us to secure valid visas to enter Poland before the military officials would consent to issuing the necessary military orders for our entrance to Berlin.

I had made several visits to the Polish Embassy in London,

but in spite of earlier hopes and promises, nothing in the way of approval had materialized. As the time for our planned departure had now become imminent, it became necessary for me to spend almost an entire day with the first secretary and the consul general. No telephone contact with Warsaw being yet in operation, the officials in London had to rely upon a shortwave radio receiver to communicate with their superiors in Warsaw. Because of technical difficulties they were not able to establish any contact until several hours after the embassy had closed its business day, but they permitted me to remain behind until they could communicate directly by means of the radio.

Finally the consul general emerged from his office and announced that he had been unable to persuade his home office in Warsaw to grant us the permission we had requested.

When I asked whether we might contact his counterpart in Berlin, he advised me that there was no consulate or legation there at that time. Berlin had only a military mission, and they were not authorized to issue visas. With this information I returned to our headquarters, keenly disappointed at my failure to secure the vital permission.

President Benson met me at the door and inquired anxiously whether I had been able to get the needed permission. When I said no, he was noticeably disappointed. I sensed deeply with him that we were faced with a seemingly insurmountable problem. After a few moments of soulsearching reflection, during which neither one of us broke the silence, he said quietly but firmly, "Let me pray about it."

Some two or three hours after President Benson had retired to his room to pray, he stood in my doorway and said with a smile on his face, "Pack your bags. We are leaving for Poland in the morning!"

At first I could scarcely believe my eyes. He stood there enveloped in a beautiful glow of radiant light. His countenance shone as I imagine the Prophet Joseph's countenance shone when he was filled with the Spirit of the Lord.

Our lack of proper military orders would ordinarily have

presented an insurmountable obstacle, but after we explained the situation the air transport officials were willing for us to arrange for the orders upon our arrival in Berlin, in view of our previous visits there. We boarded the plane at 11:00 a.m.—an army C-47 transport with bucket seats on the sides.

Upon our arriving in Berlin there was some consternation expressed about the absence of the necessary military orders, but we were nevertheless able to arrange for them rather quickly. Then Brother Francis R. Gasser, who was connected with the U.S. Military Government in Berlin, took us out to the lovely villa occupied by Eugene Merrill and his wife. Brother Merrill's father was one of President Benson's close associates, Elder Joseph F. Merrill of the Council of the Twelve.

The Merrills were living in the palatial villa of the former chocolate magnate of Germany. In addition to servants who were living in comfortable quarters in an adjacent building, they had a private car and a chauffeur provided by the U.S. Headquarters. Brother Merrill explained that the reason they had so many servants (four and a gardener) was that this enabled them to furnish in a legal way much-needed employment and some additional foodstuffs to some of the people who were so desperately in need.

This villa was located on a picturesque little island at the edge of one of Berlin's lovely lakes. After dinner we took an evening stroll together and visited the former magnificent home of Dr. Josef Goebels, Propaganda Minister under the Hitler regime, which was now a mass of rubble; a beautiful home occupied by an American general; and one of the most elaborate and ornate homes I had ever seen, which was then serving as the Lakeside Officers' Club.

The Merrills provided Elder Benson and me with beautiful separate bedrooms. Every upstairs bedroom had ornate French doors opening out toward the lake and every upstairs room had a private balcony. But such luxury was to be short-lived.

The next morning (Saturday) we learned that there was only one plane a week to Warsaw—an army C-47 which carried the diplomatic pouch to our American ambassador in Warsaw. It was required to make the round trip on a single day, not being permitted to remain there overnight. We made tentative reservations to join the flight on Tuesday.

Despite the negative information we had received before leaving London, we sought out the Polish Military Mission Headquarters in the hope that they could help us obtain permission to go to Warsaw. Brother Gasser, who was invited to accompany us to Poland, went with us. It being Saturday, the office had already closed, but by knocking persistently and explaining our dilemma we were finally admitted.

The secretary of the Mission was courteous, but he assured us unmistakably that all visas had first to be cleared with Warsaw and that about fourteen days would elapse in the process, as communications between Berlin and Warsaw could only be accomplished by courier. President Benson explained that we had already secured tentative passage on the following Tuesday's plane and that a delay of two weeks was out of the question because of other pressing commitments.

Finally the general in charge emerged from a conference in his office, and the secretary explained to him our request and predicament. He too told us that he was powerless to help us; but when President Benson asked him if we might again call on him Monday morning, he graciously agreed.

On Monday as we were riding in a jeep to keep our appointment at the Polish Military Mission headquarters I asked President Benson if we were still going to Poland. Without a moment's hesitation he said yes.

Within ten minutes after our arrival at the headquarters, President Benson had secured the necessary clearances for all three of us. In spite of all the warnings both in London and Berlin that such a thing was absolutely impossible, the impossible had taken place. Again the Lord's promise had been vindicated "And they shall go forth and none shall stay them, for I the Lord have commanded them."

En route to Warsaw the following morning we had to stay within a narrow five-mile air corridor while passing over Russian-occupied territory. Because of this limitation our pilot had to plow directly through an ominous thunderhead which was directly in our flight path. As we neared the center, we were struck by a large bolt of lightning. A fireball—about the size of a basketball—bounded between the metal sides inside the plane about halfway between the pilot's cabin and our position in the plane. The air was filled with an ozone smell and the sides of the plane seemed momentarily sucked in. They returned to normal with a loud bang as the fireball disappeared.

For a few moments the plane went completely out of control, and it appeared that we might crash, yet I felt no fear. I had been promised I would return safely, but I was very interested in how the Lord would get us out of this situation. As the plane hurtled toward the ground we thought we recognized the sound of anti-aircraft fire. Fortunately the pilot was able to bring the plane under control before we reached the tree tops and we arrived at our destination without further incident.

From the air the countryside was beautiful with its yellow, gray, and green patchwork of fields, forests, and meadows threaded with rivers and highways. Hamlets and lakes appeared and disappeared. Occasionally we could observe zig-zag trenches, bomb craters, and devastated cities. The scars of war were clearly in evidence. Later we learned that many of the green fields contained nothing but green weeds.

There were no runways in sight as our crippled cargo plane approached Warsaw. We were to land in a pasture. Our pilot buzzed the airfield, which started a number of people below us chasing the cows and horses out of our pathway so they would not be struck. For smoothness, the pasture left much to be desired. What remained of the airport was nothing but a heap of rubble, but new landing strips had been commenced.

As we deplaned, we saw on the side of the plane a large area that looked as if it had been fired with a welding torch. I felt very grateful that we had been spared from what might have been a tragedy.

Mr. Gist, vice consul of the American Embassy, was on hand to meet us and took us into the city of Warsaw, where we were given a room at the Polonia Hotel—virtually the only building made reasonably habitable in the heart of this once-beautiful city. Our accommodations consisted of a single small room filled with army cots. We shared our room with seven other persons and felt most fortunate to do so. Outside were tens of thousands of Polish people who had to get along without shelter of any kind.

At the hotel we met a gentleman of the Seventh Day Adventist faith who was on a mission of mercy similar to ours. He asked President Benson what he had in mind to do during this trip and how long he expected to remain. President Benson explained that we had only one week in which to confer with leading Polish officials and to visit our scattered members in southern, eastern and northern Poland.

To this the gentleman responded: "Mr. Benson, don't you realize that we've just been through a disastrous war? Transportation in Poland is almost non-existent. I've been here over a month now, and so far I haven't even been able to get a jeep to take me beyond the city limits of Warsaw."

Before we had been in Warsaw very long it was easy to understand why it was regarded as Europe's most battered city. It had been completely and systematically gutted out. Most of the people there were living in cellars.

When the Germans took over in 1939, the city had already been damaged by their air raids. The resistance in this city gave them more trouble than that in any other city in Poland. The Germans became more and more angry. Finally, when the Polish insurrection broke loose with the encouragement of the advancing Russians, the Germans systematically sacked the city, burning out the homes block by block and pulverizing many with dynamite. Many of the inhabitants who could be seized were placed in front of their homes and shot to death. The insurrection was ill-timed and very costly—accounting for nearly 70 percent of Poland's losses—but Warsaw's inhabitants resisted until the Russians arrived.

With the exception of a battered church, there was not a wall nor a chimney left standing in the Jewish ghetto area. The people of Warsaw were, in the main, poorly clad, hungry and unkempt. Paradoxically, one could buy all the food—fresh or canned—and all the clothing, furs, silver, etc., one wished in Warsaw. These articles were there in abundance—if one had the money. Prices ranged from 6 American dollars for a meal to 700 American dollars—18,000 Polish slotty—for a pair of riding boots.

People lined the main streets with armfuls of American cigarettes, American canned juices, vegetables, meats, etc., seeking to sell these goods at black-market prices. Misery was all round. Yet the few night clubs and cocktail lounges which had been restored and reopened were ablaze with light and resounded with music and the voices of their patrons.

President Benson conferred with the American ambassador, Arthur Bliss Lane, and was cordially received. Ambassador Lane was a very warm personal friend of President J. Reuben Clark, Jr., and accorded President Benson every courtesy. He agreed to contact the various Polish officials' we needed to see and prepare the way for us to handle our business.

That evening we made a short tour of the city. I had never seen such filth, so many beggars, so many unkempt people. Realizing the conditions under which they were having to live, one could understand in part why such a condition existed.

The people generally seemed to be too destitute to buy anything, so American relief supplies which they received they sold for the highest possible price in hopes of being able to buy some staples like bread and potatoes. We saw every type of article imaginable in shop windows and on the streets. American cigarettes were being sold everywhere by small boys and girls at about $2.50 per package. They called them "Papyroczy." Many of the small children selling cigarettes and canned goods had part of a canned goods carton suspended by rope around their shoulders. Quite a number were on crutches, with one leg or a hand missing—or in some cases part of a face.

We walked through block after block of the most desolate rubble I had yet seen. The farther we walked, the more overpowering the feelings of depression and sadness became. Finally we turned around and returned to our crowded room for the night.

Russian soldiers were everywhere in evidence. Polish soldiers were also numerous—at least, young men wearing

Polish military clothing. They were all dirty, unkempt, and armed to the teeth.

We checked on transportation for our trip to Wroclaw (Breslau) and Zelbak (Selbongen), and were able to arrange for use of an UNRRA (United Nations Relief and Rehabilitation Agency) jeep for the trip to Zelbak (Selbongen) at the end of the week, but plane transportation to Wroclaw (Breslau) was unavailable. However, through the assistance of the Minister of Transportation we were able to arrange for two tickets on the overnight train to Wroclaw (Breslau) that evening. President Benson was still hopeful he could arrange for plane transportation in the morning and meet us at our destination (which he finally did).

The railway depot was filled with crowds and crowds of filthy, squalid, emaciated people. Then when our train pulled in Brother Gasser and I were heartsick. (Fortunately we had solicited the aid of two Polish guards to get us on our part of the train.) With the exception of one dilapidated coach car, it consisted of foul-smelling box cars—freight cars and cattle cars.

The people fought fiercely to get into these cars—mothers with tiny babies, expectant mothers, old and young men, women and children. They jammed themselves painfully into, on top of, outside, and in between the box cars. And it rained for nearly the entire thirteen-hour trip to Wroclaw (Breslau).

Most of the people boarding the train appeared to be hauling all of their earthly possessions with them. Many of them probably were refugees (a commonplace sight throughout the occupied areas). There was no modesty or privacy available for them, no restroom facilities of any kind.

We had a dirty third-class coach with wooden seats for our comfort. There were no windows or ventilation. We were seated next to the horrible-smelling toilet facilities, all of which contributed to the unpleasantness of our journey. Our compartment was crowded to capacity. But in comparison with the rest of the people on the train, we rode like kings.

Along the way the next morning we noted the complete absence of cattle, horses, and other livestock (as in Germany). We learned that the Russians had taken most of these into their own homeland. Farm machinery of all kinds, work stock, and fertilizers were also practically nonexistent. As a result, thousands of acres of land were idle and the cultivated lands were sadly neglected and full of weeds.

Apart from Warsaw itself and a few other places, the cities in Poland itself, in contrast to the German areas taken over, were only slightly damaged. The factories appeared to have suffered little damage, but again we were told that the Russians had removed much of the machinery and hence many factories were unable to operate.

Wroclaw (Breslau) was a terrible sight—it was almost as badly hit as Warsaw. The railway station was teeming with humanity: persons sleeping; mothers changing their babies' diapers; refugees sitting exhausted amid their belongings. The deplorable plight of these people cannot be adequately described. I thought to myself, "God help these fleeing refugees and displaced persons!"

Brother Gasser and I found our way to the squalid home of the branch president. We hadn't been there ten minutes before a Russian soldier knocked at the door demanding to be admitted. The branch president was not home and his wife refused to open the door. She had much of her furniture stacked against the door to discourage forced entry.

From the conversation at the time and the facts gathered later, we learned that this soldier had come to haul her away from her family of four children to engage in forced labor—for which she would have received neither pay nor meals. As the soldier left he assured this good woman that he would return in the morning with others to take her to work whether she liked it or not.

At that time the German saints in Poland had virtually no security. They were expected to subsist by selling all their belongings and purchasing food on the "black market" at outrageous prices. Meanwhile their homes were subjected to frequent pilfering. Everything the marauding Russian and Polish conquerors wanted they took. German women were being raped; German men were being whipped and beaten, imprisoned and killed.

Our saints were in desperate straits. They had been forced to sell every piece of available clothing (except what they had on their bodies), all the household belongings they had been able to hide from plundering bands, and their keepsakes, jewelry, etc. Virtually all of their material possessions had been stripped from them.

President Benson arrived by plane shortly before noon and at the airport met the Vice President of the City of Wroclaw (Breslau) and the Director of Newspaper Publicity. The latter was kind enough to take him by car into the city.

On the plane—one that looked very much in need of major repairs—President Benson had had to sit on a threelegged stool placed in the aisle. As the pilot began his takeoff, the stool and its passenger slid to the rear bulkhead. When the plane landed, President Benson found himself hurled almost into the cockpit of the plane.

Brother Gasser and I had secured hotel rooms for the night and were trying to arrange transportation for the next day. Consequently we did not meet President Benson until 6 p.m. when we held a meeting with the saints. Meanwhile he had constructive conferences with the Vice President and the newsman. Both pledged their full cooperation. They agreed to help our people move to the British Zone of Germany, assuring us that they would give as much special consideration as possible. In addition, they agreed to advertise in the newspapers for our members to register with them in Wroclaw (Breslau) or with us in London in order that the work of finding our scattered members could be expedited.

There were forty-six people at the meeting that evening—the same meetinghall they occupied before the war. It was badly damaged but still usable. We had an emotion-laden meeting and agreed to advise the branch president the next morning whether or not the saints could be permitted to leave or to remain behind as Polish citizens. Any Polish citizenship was considered to be only a temporary expedient fraught with many possibilities for discrimination.

After the meeting we visited a special garden the saints had planted amid the ruins. They had received permission to retain their harvested vegetables. We learned that most of our 134 members living there at that time were receiving a helpful amount of produce from this unusual garden. To this we added the small but welcome hundred pounds of foodstuffs we had brought along from Berlin and Warsaw with the hope that it would help some of them until they could arrange to leave for Germany.

We retired that night with heavy hearts.

We met with the branch president and three other brethren the next morning. President Benson had prayed about the matter of their removal and now outlined specific steps to be taken. We left 10,000 slotty with them ($100.00) so that the branch president could have some limited funds with which to assist the most needy.

I left to board the bus for Katowice and arranged to have the driver wait until President Benson could arrive. Meanwhile he and Brother Gasser and the branch president paid a final visit to the Vice President of Wroclaw. While they were there it was decided that Brother Gasser should remain an extra day to follow through on various matters dealing with the ultimate removal of our members from this area.

Later as we were riding on the bus to Katowice we noticed hundreds of women along the road working as section hands on the railways, as members of road construction crews, as lumberjacks, and in various other types of back-breaking work. Many of these were apparently Germans. We noticed that women were doing most of the heavy work.

We observed that not a village in all of Silesia (formerly German territory) had been spared the desolation of war. However, as soon as we crossed the borders into old Poland, the cities were almost untouched, the factories and blast furnaces were in full swing. What a contrast just to cross the border! It reminded me of Czechoslovakia. During our trip we saw hundreds of Russian soldiers, all dirty and heavily armed.

When we arrived in Katowice—a city of about 350,000 people—it was late afternoon. The railroad station presented a sickening scene similar to the one we had witnessed in Warsaw and Wroclaw. A quick check revealed that there were no busses or trains available to take us to Warsaw, so President Benson and I went our separate ways to try to find some kind of transportation. We agreed to meet at a designated corner in about half an hour. He would try to locate an International Red Cross office while I searched for other possibilities.

I had walked along one of the streets about three blocks—and it was already getting quite dark—when two young teen-age girls approached me. One of them spoke shyly to me in Polish. Since I could not understand her, I smiled and shrugged my shoulders. Then her companion spoke to me in German, which I could understand, and asked: "Aren't you an American?"

"Yes, I am," was my reply.

She glanced back at her companion and asked, "Aren't you a Mormon missionary?"

I was delighted to assure her that I was. Her question came as a complete surprise. To the best of our knowledge we had no members living in Poland except for those Germans who had not yet been moved to one of the occupied zones in Germany proper. It transpired that these girls were two of our German refugee saints who had been left behind, not knowing whether their families were still alive. During our brief conversation, they learned of our dilemma and confirmed the fact that there was no public transportation available at that time from Katowice to Warsaw.

The younger of the two girls spoke up. "A few minutes ago I saw a British lorry {truck} stop at a restaurant about four blocks from here." She pointed out the direction. "Two British officers got out to get a bite to eat," she continued. "Why don't you check with them? They may be going to Warsaw."

I thanked them for this suggestion and hurried to locate these officers. (I never saw these girls again. Why did they pick me out of the masses of people in this large city? Why did they have the answer we needed? For me this was but another evidence of the Lord's continuing promise that "they shall go forth and none shall stay them, for I the Lord have commanded them.")

The British officers were seated at a table near the front window of the restaurant, just finishing their scanty meal. When I introduced myself and explained our problems, they said that they were driving on to Warsaw but that they were not permitted to take any passengers. They were both assigned to UNRRA. They would be driving through territory where many trucks were being hijacked by desperate people, they said, and they did not wish to accept responsibility for endangering other people's lives.

I assured them that we were unafraid and were perfectly willing to assume the risks and discomforts involved. They finally agreed to take us not only to Warsaw but also to some neighboring cities where our mission records indicated we might find one or two isolated Church families.

Soon President Benson and I were on our way to Gliwice (Gleiwitz). We were unable to contact any of the Church members directly, whether in Gleiwitz or Beuthen or Hindenburg, but a friend, whose daughter was a member, gave us a good accounting of those still in the area. We left our remaining food supplies and some money, which she agreed to pass on to the presiding authorities. Then we headed for Warsaw.

In spite of the warning we had received of marauding bands and hijackings, we drove through the night until nearly 3 a.m. and arrived without incident. While we had rather cramped quarters in the back of the truck, we were filled with gratitude for the kindness of those who made this memorable trip possible.

We had arranged to leave by jeep for East Prussia by 12 noon. Since it was raining quite hard and we had not had much sleep, President Benson decided we should wait until the following day (Sunday) at which time Brother Gasser would have returned and could join us. So we requested the driver of the UNRRA jeep to return at 9 a.m. the following morning.

Since we had time we could use productively, we called on a number of leading Polish officials. We especially enjoyed our visit with Stanislaw Mikolajczyk, First Vice President and Minister of Agriculture. During the war he had served as acting Premier of Poland in exile, directing activities from London. Since he was then the leader of the political party opposed to the Russian-oriented puppet government, he told us that his stay in Poland might be short-lived.

That afternoon we visited the famous Warsaw Ghetto. It was

a terrible sight. Before the war Warsaw had about 1,250,000 people, of whom 350,000 were Jewish. The Jews lived in this Ghetto section, and when the Germans arrived they forced the Jews to build a solid wall all around it, including fortifications, etc. Then they cut the Jews off from the outside and forced them to live as best they could on what they could produce within their confined complex. To increase their hardships, an additional 200,000 Jews were shipped in to join them.

We were assured by some of those whom we contacted that many of the Polish people were in favor of this policy. Any Jews trying to escape from this virtual prison were shot. Later this section was used as a proving ground for every type of weapon—planes, tanks, flame throwers, etc. Some of the inhabitants escaped through the sewers. The rest were all killed. On April 19, 1943, the Warsaw Ghetto rose in arms Finally put down on May 16, it marked one of the most heroic and at the same time most tragic battles in man's fight against Hitlerism. It was carried on by a handful of men and women who, cut off from the world by the Ghetto walls, and aware that they were doomed to perish, seized arms to show the world how free people could fight and die.

The Warsaw Ghetto uprising was not an event isolated from Poland's total war effort against the Nazi invasion. Preparing for it months ahead, the Jews were receiving arms and ammunition from democratic groups of underground Poland. At the time of the uprising, the Jewish Underground Military Organization issued an appeal to the Poles in which it referred to its action as "a fight for our human, social and national honor," under the slogan of "Brotherhood of arms and blood of fighting Poland," for "our freedom and yours." The noted Polish author, Stanislaw Ryszard Dobrowolski, called the uprising "the Thermopylae of fighting Warsaw."

When the insurrection came, this area was completely leveled by the Nazis—an area well over a square mile in which the only object left standing was a burned-out church in the middle. Not only were there no walls left standing, but hardly a brick remaining was usable, so complete had been the destruction.

Our driver of the quaint "droshka" (horse-drawn carriage) volunteered that there were still over 200,000 bodies buried beneath the rubble. The stench of decaying human flesh was sickening. It was the most desolate sight we had yet witnessed— a testimony of the barbaric cruelty and inhumanity meted out to these defenseless people.

As dusk began to fall we saw a sea of rats and mice scurrying across these ruins in horrifying waves, and we were told they were feasting upon the dead bodies. Our driver also told us that some seven thousand families still were hiding and living in cellar areas among these ruins—a thing that seemed incredible to us. This area was being sprayed with DDT from planes in an effort to prevent a recurrence of the bubonic plague which took the lives of one-third of Europe's population several centuries ago and was known as the Black Death.

Upon his arrival early the next morning, Brother Gasser reported that he had attracted considerable attention in Katowice. People were astonished to see a man in the uniform of the United States. Brother Gasser jokingly suggested that they apparently had not been informed that all Americans had not been killed in the war!

Brother Gasser and the Polish driver of our jeep recommended that we eat breakfast before leaving for Zelbak (Selbongen), but President Benson reminded them that it was Fast Sunday and that we should therefore forego eating. Our Polish driver was quite unhappy over this verdict, but he and Brother Gasser did not realize that neither President Benson nor I had eaten a meal since Wednesday.

We were soon on our way in our jeep for a 376-kilometer trip (235 miles). We bounced over the cobblestone roads at 45 to 50 miles an hour, hurrying through bombed villages at a speed unhealthful both for their inhabitants and for the jeep occupants. We could not make our driver (who had been in England eight years and understood English perfectly when he wished to) understand that he should be more cautious and less hasty.

The weather was quite fair, but there was a strong westerly wind that wouldn't let us forget we were in a jeep. The top kept flapping so much that we finally took it down. Then we were really fanned by the breeze. Suddenly it began to rain in torrents, so we hurriedly raised the top again. Since I was on the windward side of the jeep, my raincoat became thoroughly soaked. The stiff breeze was too much for the rain-soaked top. One of the supports broke and a long tear resulted. The rest of our trip was made with the top down—rain or shine.

Our driver kept blowing his horn without provocation and then would see how close he could come to people, to horses, and to other cars. (We were told that this was typical of Polish drivers.) A couple of times he frightened horses so badly that we feared they would jump right into the jeep. It didn't matter which side of the road the people or the vehicles were on—when he had blown his horn, he expected them to get completely off the road. He would head straight toward them if they did not drive into the barrow pit quickly enough. It made all of us a bit nervous and somewhat unhappy with the driver.

When noontime rolled around, the driver began looking for a place to eat. Again President Benson suggested that we not stop, since we still had a considerable distance to drive. I saw then how angry the driver was becoming due to this (as he supposed) lack of consideration for the driver and his welfare. I began to realize why he was driving so angrily and erratically.

Except for these problems, the trip was uneventful. We had to pass numerous sentry stations, and several times we got off the main road due to the lack of adequate road signs. Everywhere we went we got salutes from the people as we passed. The highways were fringed with trees and stones painted white. The fields were beautifully colored as we entered what was formerly East Prussia.

Here and there a bunker reared its concrete face and old neutralized roadblocks appeared. Men and women—mostly women—were in the fields cutting, raking, and tying grain into sheaves by hand. During the entire trip we saw only two machines for such work—two outmoded tractors and an old hand-fed threshing machine.

As we entered what was formerly East Prussia, we noted that every village, large or small, was badly shelled, bombed, and gutted out with fire. Along the way were dozens of wrecked and burned-out tanks, trucks, cannons, planes, and other equipment. This must have been a fierce battleground. We lost the road twice and took back-country roads as detours to the main highways. Only a jeep could have made it on some of the stretches of road we traveled.

Not a sign of life was upon the streets as we entered the little village of Zelbak (Selbongen), East Prussia, in our faithful jeep. We thought it rather strange because it was a beautiful day to be out for a Sunday stroll and enjoying the cool summer breezes. Proceeding to the further end of the village we spied the branch chapel—the only Church-owned chapel in all of what was formerly Germany—and upon alighting from our vehicle we asked the only woman in sight if this was the Mormon chapel and where we might find the branch president.

We had spotted the woman hiding behind a large tree. Her expression was one of fear as we stopped, but upon learning who we were she greeted us with tears of gratitude and joy. She was one of our refugee members, formerly from Cologne, Germany, who escaped to the East when the Allied troops invaded France and Germany and then found herself trapped as the Russian armies swept in from the East.

All was quiet as we approached the home of the branch president, Brother Adolf Kruska. His home was next to the chapel. In fact, the chapel had been built upon a piece of his property. This good sister knocked on his door, but no one stirred. Then she called out: "It's all right. The elders have arrived from Zion!"

We could hear the safety latch being removed from the doors, and in a few moments women, young girls and children appeared almost miraculously, crying and laughing excitedly, each one trying to express their unbounded joy and happiness. Within minutes the cry went from house to house, "The brethren are here! The brethren are here!" Soon we found ourselves surrounded by about fifty of the happiest people we had ever seen.

Having seen our strange jeep approaching with what they feared to be Russian or Polish soldiers, they had abandoned the streets as if by magic. Likewise, when they learned of our true identity and mission, the village became alive with joyous women and children—women and children, because only two of our former twenty-nine priesthood holders remained.

That morning in fast and testimony meeting over one hundred saints had assembled together to bear their testimonies and to petition Almighty God in song, in fasting and prayer, to be merciful to them and let the elders again come to visit them. Our sudden and unheralded arrival, after almost complete isolation from Church and mission headquarters since early 1943, was the long-awaited answer, so wonderful that they could scarcely believe their good fortune. Never had we seen love and gratitude more deeply expressed. Nothing would do but to have another meeting!

Meanwhile our Polish driver was bewildered. Since we had now arrived at this destination, he expected us at last to have something to eat, but President Benson suggested that we wait until after the meeting with the saints!

While the people were assembling from all directions, Brother Gasser went with the driver to Olszytn (Allenstein) to replenish our dwindling gas supply and bring in a member of the branch presidency who lived about nine kilometers from the meeting-house. We learned later that this brother had had all his clothing and possessions confiscated and that one of the sisters lent him an extra woman's slip so that he could come to the meeting.

Within the hour 104 friends and members were crowded into the plain but attractive chapel to enjoy the Spirit of the Lord which was poured out in a marvelous manner. As the meeting proceeded, two Polish officers entered with a self-assured air, much to the discomfort of the members present. President Benson had already begun speaking. At first these two men were rather discourteous, but before President Benson had finished speaking their attitude seemed to change greatly and they remained in the service until the closing song. I had the privilege of addressing the group after translating for Elder Benson.

After the closing prayer (now that the Polish officers had departed), the saints called out as with one voice, "Let's hold another meeting!" What a wonderful spirit!

After the meeting, Brother Kruska took us to his home and provided us with food and feather beds. We had inquired for an inn and had actually found one partially intact, but as it was closed we were forced to accept the hospitality of the saints even though we did not feel too happy about their giving us their beds.

As we met together in the home, we began to learn something of what had been happening. Since the end of hostilities our saints in the territories ceded to Poland had become a despised, persecuted, and unwanted people because of their German nationality. They had endured the most shocking cruelties and bestialities.

One of our faithful brethren was shot down in cold blood by the invading troops from the East because he could not produce the cigarettes for which they had asked him. His mother, who ran to lift up his lifeless body from the pool of blood in which it lay, was driven away at the point of bayonets and threatened with death. As this forlorn mother comforted his grief-stricken wife—the mother of two lovely children—these soldiers whipped and flogged the two women so severely that they were unable to lie down comfortably for two weeks.

Since that day women and girls—some of them just approaching adolescence—had been repeatedly ravished. One of the mothers was forced at the point of a gun to remain in the room and watch her daughter being ravished by a group of ten soldiers. Another young girl, not quite twelve years old, had been raped several times. One of the married sisters was ravished three times in a single night. Meanwhile her husband, who had been on crutches for some time as a semi-invalid, was snatched from his sickbed and deported to Siberia, never to be heard from again. This mother now had a Russian baby to care for, as a result of this experience, in addition to two children by her deported husband.

Until the last two months the saints had been in daily fear of their lives. Their homes had been repeatedly entered at night and plundered. Everything the marauders desired had been confiscated. Their lusts had run rampant. Men, women, and children had been taken from homes, never to be seen again.

As we were going to Brother Kruska's home, he showed us the fresh grave by the side of the chapel where his son, who didn't have the cigarettes to give the invading troops, was buried. There were still freshly cut flowers on the grave to remind us how recently this scene had taken place on the steps of the little chapel.

Since the Russian armies, withdrawing in favor of the Polish troops, had taken practically all cattle, horses, sheep, hogs, and fowl with them, livestock was scarce. Some families had managed to retain one or two chickens, but many of these had since been confiscated. Nearly the entire egg production had been requisitioned by the occupying troops, and the present shortage of feed made it questionable whether remaining poultry could be kept alive.

At one time our people concealed their chickens in large water-tight metal containers filled partially with large stones to sink them in water. Having lowered them with ropes into the adjacent lake, at night they would bring these containers to the surface, open the lids to refresh the air supply, give the chickens some rye or other grain, and occasionally find an egg. During the winter they cut holes through the ice on the lake in order to preserve their poultry by this means.

Clothing and valuables had been ruthlessly confiscated as well. Many of the people buried their belongings in shallow containers under the sod. The military forces went from lot to lot with long probing rods in an effort to find them. Meanwhile the people had removed most of the containers to other locations. If anything was found, it was shipped to the East.

Most German men and women were forced to work eight to twelve hours a day, many of them receiving neither money nor food in exchange. Those who served as gang bosses or foremen were paid the equivalent of forty cents a day. Ration cards allowing people to buy certain food items at regular prices had not been honored. This necessitated purchasing food and other articles at exorbitant prices on the "black market."

Our saints were facing a most critical period. One brother, after being repeatedly plundered, was again accosted for further plunder. When his tormentors learned that the coat and pants he was wearing had been given him by a friend to cover his nakedness, following the last plundering in which everything had been taken, and that he was wearing a borrowed woman's slip as a shirt, they felt ashamed and had since ceased making him a target of their depredations.

These people were but a few of the innocent victims of war. The victorious armies, ever mindful of the inhuman atrocities inflicted upon their countrymen by the enemy, their hearts now filled with hatred and the spirit of revenge, became fiends in human form. They sought to justify their own villainous and cowardly acts by the dastardly treatment previously meted out by their enemies.

We had brought some items of food with us which we were able to secure in Warsaw from our embassy commissary. These, together with a couple of eggs the Kruskas had and some rye bread, constituted our meal. The rye had been ground with ordinary rocks and there seemed to be a liberal amount of finely ground rock mixed with the rye. Our Polish driver remarked that this was the longest period he had ever gone without food in his entire lifetime.

Most of our members in this small community owned their own lands and homes. The lands had been turned over to the Polish people coming into this territory. The homes would subsequently be confiscated as soon as their German occupants could be repatriated—all without any compensation. Some of our saints still had a few small pieces of unclaimed land on which they were raising potatoes and rye. They planted, harvested, threshed and ground the rye, then used it for bread.

This branch had carried on regular meetings throughout the entire war years with one or two brief interruptions. Twenty-seven of their male membership were missing as prisoners of war, as fatalities, or as slave laborers deported into Russia or Siberia. The two remaining brethren had succeeded marvelously in keeping the spirit of unity and love among the saints. Their faith and devotion was a testimony to me of the power of the gospel of Jesus Christ in a person's life.

The branch members held no bitterness or resentment toward those who had inflicted the injustices upon them. They continued to manifest only love and compassion.

We stayed overnight in Brother Kruska's home in fairly comfortable beds. I don't know where he or his family slept, but I know that our comfort was their only concern.

Before returning to Warsaw the following morning, President Benson dedicated the grave of the brother so recently buried by the side of the chapel. He also gave helpful instructions concerning the future and left with the members 21,500 slotty ($215.00) to assist them with some of their immediate needs. Then he invited Brother Kruska to ride with us to Olsztyn (Allenstein) where we met with more Polish officials and received the same reception and the same word: no one is yet permitted to leave. They agreed, however, to see to it that our saints would be protected in their homes. In turn we agreed to help financially and otherwise with their resettlement should the decision that they leave be forthcoming.

Upon arriving in Zelbak (Selbongen) we had been just about out of gas. Brother Gasser was subsequently able to buy our gallons (but only on the "black market"—there being no regular gas stations available) at $2.50 per gallon This was sufficient to take us to Olsztyn (Allenstein), but not sufficient to drive the branch president back to Selbongen, so he was forced to walk the twelve to fourteen miles home. We were disappointed that we could not return him to his home in our jeep.

Upon our arrival at the Warsaw airport we met the gentleman who, on the day of our arrival, had told us there was no way we could travel in Poland. He inquired where we had been, since he had not seen us around Warsaw. We informed him that we had been visiting with our people in southern, eastern, and northern Poland.

Then he asked how we had managed to get around. We replied that we had used trains, busses, planes, jeeps, and even a "droshka" (horsedrawn buggy, something like the ones used in Grand Central Park in New York City). President Benson explained that we had visited our various groups of members, had contacted Polish governmental officials wherever we had gone, and were now ready to return to Berlin and London.

I shall never forget the look of utter incredulity on the man's face as he exclaimed, "I can't believe it. That's impossible!"

But we knew that with the Lord "all things are possible."

chapter eleven

The Changing Scene

When President Benson returned to London he was greeted by the official word that Elder Alma Sonne had been appointed to replace him. Because of this news and the drastic adjustments that it foreshadowed, much of President Benson's remaining time was involved in administrative activities.

This plus my own resultant workload left not much time for relaxation. One evening, however, we drove out to the British Mission home to deliver a number of used clothing packages from Canada and the United States for the use of our British saints. After a good dinner, we went over on the "common" (an unfenced green space set off for recreation in larger British cities) and enjoyed the tail-end of a baseball game. President Benson entered right into the spirit of things, batting the ball, running the bases, catching and fielding. All of those present were profoundly impressed that a modern apostle could be just as good a sport as the Prophet Joseph Smith had been in his day. I acted as catcher for both teams. This was the first relaxation we had had in a long time.

President Benson received a telegram from the First Presidency asking us to postpone indefinitely our scheduled trip to Palestine and South Africa, at least until after President Sonne arrived, at which time further consideration would be given to the matter.

We had spent many hours during the past four months in securing permissions, visas, plane tickets, hotel reservations, etc., for the various countries concerned, and now we had to undo it all. It was a complicated task to handle all these cancellations and refunds, but I tried to take it as all part of a day's work.

What would happen to our saints who were then in Syria and Lebanon was a matter of grave concern to us. Considerable pressure was being brought to bear to have them return to their former homeland in Armenia, which was now a part of the Soviet Union. (Not many months passed before the saints accepted the invitation to return to the Soviet Union. They were granted full rights of citizenship.)

When we received the latest copy of the South African Mission's publication, *Cumorah's Southern Messenger,* the front page had a large picture of President Benson and myself and the headline, "President Benson Coming." Reading this article just about broke President Benson's spirit. He felt so keenly what a disappointment the people in the South African Mission would experience at the change of plan, as also those in the Palestine-Syrian Mission who had been so anxious to have counsel in view of an impending Near East crisis. I believe that this cancellation was the biggest single disappointment we experienced during our entire time in Europe.

About this time we ran across a feature article by Louis Hagen of Britain's *Sunday Express* entitled "How the Cigarette Rules Germany." It recorded the author's observations on a trip he had recently made to Berlin. From our own experience, we felt that it accurately portrayed the situation then existing. Because of our LDS Word of Wisdom and the facts which have since become generally accepted on the health dangers of cigarette addiction, I include here some brief excerpts from the article.

> Germany is a land almost run on cigarettes. Seventy-five per cent of everyday crime in the country is traceable to cigarettes....

> You can't throw a cigarette stump away without someone diving into the road to pick it up. Nearly everyone does it, no matter of what social position.

> This was brought home to me when my own cousin, a member of a very wealthy and exceedingly straight-laced family, told me that he often walks for miles hoping to pick up a few cigarettes.

Women do it too. They walk along the main streets and wait for the cigarette ends to be thrown out of the jeeps Some people travel all day in the tubes [subways] to pick up the cigarette stumps dropped by the Americans.

Many women, even those with children sell their ration cards to buy cigarettes.

All services and all work have to be paid for in cigarettes…shoes soled…your trousers pressed. There is nothing at all, from butter, hams, shoes, to liquor, that you cannot get for cigarettes. Money has no pull at all.

A cigarette is worth rather more than a workman's daily wage.

A large percentage of the German cigarette buyers are women. At times, they become quite maniacal, selling their children's food, their belongings and even themselves to get cigarettes.

One cannot possibly imagine the lengths to which people who lack tobacco will go to get a smoke. It is far worse than hunger.

If you are hungry and smoke, you don't feel so hungry. But hunger intensifies tenfold the desire to smoke. Most German people are usually hungry.

At the moment, the men of Berlin get 12 very inferior cigarettes (a kind of straw mixture, grown in Germany) a month, and the women get six.

If anyone thinks that Germany is not yet punished sufficiently, they might suggest the withdrawal of all cigarettes. That would be worse than any other punishment that could be devised.

In sending a copy of this article to the First Presidency and commenting upon it, President Benson told them how few days before, while standing on a street corner in Frankfurt, he observed two or three GIs waiting for a bus. As the bus approached, one of the men flipped his cigarette butt into the gutter. Almost before it hit the pavement, two Germans who had been standing by, waiting for the GI to finish his smoke, jumped to get the cigarette butt. As one laid hits hand on the butt, the other placed his foot on the hand over the butt and crushed it so badly with his heel that he forced the man to give up. He then stooped over and picked up the remains of the cigarette.

A letter from the First Presidency arrived telling me in general terms how long I might expect my mission to continue. It stated:

> We received with great pleasure your letter of August 21 telling us of the joy and the spiritual upbuilding which has come to you from your working along with President Ezra Taft Benson. We, with you, feel that the Lord has been near to him and has abundantly blessed him in his labors. We have great joy in the love which has been extended to him by the saints and know that it is not misplaced. We are exceedingly grateful to our Heavenly Father for the access which he has obtained and the good feeling which has been engendered among those in authority with whom he has come in contact. This has been a great aid to his work. We feel that in all this you have been of great assistance.
>
> With reference to yourself, as we have already advised President Benson, we shall ask him to remain with Brother Sonne until the latter has familiarized himself with the work and its problems and has met the people. We are sure it would be a great blessing if you would remain at least that long with the Brethren, and we will ask Brother Sonne to consult with you and with President Benson about the length of time you might remain after President Benson returns. We feel that it would not be fair or wise to ask you to continue indefinitely in the mission, or for any great term, in view of the service you have already rendered the Church, and in view of your young family.
>
> Our hearts likewise go out in gratitude to you for your loyal devoted service, not only to the cause itself, but to President Benson. We can see from his reports as well as from his statements made to us that he values your service most highly and that you have been of great assistance to him. We repeat, we are thankful to our Heavenly Father for this service.
>
> Faithfully yours,
>
> George Albert Smith
> J. Reuben Clark, Jr.
> David O. McKay
> The First Presidency

During this period I was invited to speak in a sacrament meeting of the South London Branch. I had tentatively decided to speak on prayer, but it turned out differently. When I reached the lectern I enjoyed a unique experience. I felt that I was standing to one side of myself, perhaps eight feet away. I had the sensation of looking at myself at the speaker's stand and wondering what I was going to say.

As the first thought began to be expressed I was thrilled and amazed, never having heard such a thought expressed so clearly before. It was as though I was the most interested listener in the audience. I had no awareness of making any effort to speak.

When the first idea was concluded, I recall saying to myself, "Well, that was interesting, but where do you go from here?"

Then the next thought evolved, and the next, and so on to the end of the talk. It answered many questions on which I had been thinking and searching for several years; and it opened up new spiritual insights.

I had no particularly unusual feelings as I returned to my seat. It was sufficient to realize that somehow I and my body sat down together. My heart was thrilled to overflowing as I realized that it was not I who had been speaking but that, in some manner that I don't quite understand, the power of the Holy Ghost was speaking through me and light, knowledge, and understanding were thereby being flooded in upon my soul.

As I was speaking, I had the keen realization that unlimited power was surging through my being. I felt like a railway engineer at the throttle of a powerful locomotive. I felt that I needed only to turn the throttle to unleash unlimited divine power. Little wonder, therefore, that afterwards when I was asked to bless two of the members present, I felt that there was no limit to the blessing each could receive.

The first of these was a sister in her seventh month of pregnancy who had been bleeding so profusely that both she and her husband feared she might lose the baby prematurely. As I confirmed the anointing, I again felt the tremendous surge of power I have mentioned, and I knew that she would be healed from that very moment. (She later confirmed that she was immediately healed.)

The second person was a three-year-old boy from Scotland. He had been a deaf mute since birth. Now his Parents had brought him to London for a special blessing. One of the brethren anointed his head with oil, and as I placed my hands upon his head to seal the anointing and to give him a blessing, I felt that the Lord's power was present in such abundance that there was no question about his being healed instantly.

Before I could say a word, I was told by the Spirit, "This young boy could be healed this very night if his parents would lose the hatred which they have in their hearts." I was decidedly shocked and troubled, because I had never before met this family and did not want to question their attitude. But I was restrained from sealing the anointing.

After a moment's pause, I removed my hands from the boy's head and said to his parents, "What is it that you hate so deeply?"

They looked startled. Then the husband said, "We can't tell you."

"I don't need to know," I replied, "but as I placed my hands upon your son's head, I was assured that he might be healed this very night and be restored to you whole if you will only lose the hatred which you have in your hearts."

After some troubled glances back and forth between the couple, the husband again spoke. "Well, if that is the case," he said, "our son will have to go through life as he is, because we won't give up our hating!"

I felt that I had been prevented from pronouncing a blessing that might have resulted in the salvation of the entire family. This experience taught me a profound lesson

Some of the members were still waiting until these two administrations had been attended to. One of them came forward and said: "As you were speaking, I saw you enveloped with a beautiful white light and a spirit standing near you on the right side. You truly spoke by inspiration tonight."

I thanked this good sister for her observation and was caused to marvel because it so nearly described the experience I had had.

Three weeks later in the same branch I assisted in blessing a sister who was having to undergo a mastoid operation. I felt that the spirit of healing was very strongly present but that there was a lack of receptiveness on the part of the sister.

During this period there was held a British mission-wide conference at Birmingham. Elder Benson and I attended two sessions in the afternoon, both of which were overflowing with the Spirit of the Lord. The audience seemed to feel the Spirit as I did during my brief remarks. President Benson spoke in the last session and gave the saints much sound advice.

Some had predicted that there would only be about two hundred in attendance and that two mission-wide conferences could not be held successfully in a single year. Whereas we had had between four hundred and five hundred attend the meetings in Rochdale earlier that year at the first missionwide conference since the war, we had between five hundred and six hundred at Birmingham. Britain was moving ahead!

One evening, President Benson and I had the rare experience of attending a movie. A British film called "The Magic Bow," portrayed the life of Paganini—perhaps the greatest violinist who ever lived. All the violin solos in the film were played by Yehudi Menuhin. The music and the beautiful story lifted us noticeably in our feelings. We walked home in silence. As we prepared to retire, President Benson said: "You will have to forgive me for coming all the way home without speaking. There is so much talking in the world today and so little time for meditation."

My own feelings were in complete agreement with that.

One morning President Benson suggested that we take time to see some of the sights of London. Away we went in the car, down streets large and small, until we came to Petticoat Lane. This section was notorious as a Sunday hangout for pickpockets preying on the crowds thronging the outdoor stands and markets. The outdoor vendors sold all kinds of things along the squalid streets—everything from fish to wearing apparel, jewelry, lovely porcelain, and items that were simply "catch-pennies." Even on this Wednesday there was considerable activity, and we alternately enjoyed the sights and endured the odors. It was a most pleasant diversion.

Our next stop was the British Museum. The Museum had been closed during the war, and its treasures removed from the dangers of air raids. Only one section had been opened for public inspection since the war ended. The famous "golden plates" with the three rings running through them—a description similar to the one we have of the Book of Mormon plates—had not yet been put on exhibition, but the chief custodian described them to us in some detail. He then showed us many examples of beautiful and dainty gold-leaf work, paper-thin golden tablets, etc. He explained that hundreds of years before Christ, gold was one of the commonest metals used for recording things of lasting worth.

Five or six weeks before President Benson expected to return to his home in Salt Lake City, he wrote a special fare well message and testimony for inclusion in the various mission publications. As I typed it I recognized it as one of the most stirring and inspirational documents I had read in a long time, reminiscent of earlier Church leaders in its forthright spirit, its boldness, and its unbounded love and humility. It came from the depths of a heart overflowing with the pure love of God and a testimony tested and found to be valiant.

One evening I was invited to dine upstairs with our landlady Miss Heather Price and Sir Frederick and Lady James. For the first forty-five minutes Miss Price and I chatted until the other two guests arrived. She was very much interested in why Elder Benson and I were in England, what we were doing, etc. For half an hour I told her the story of the restoration of the gospel and why Christianity in general was failing to imbue the citizens of Britain with the power to change their lives sufficiently to insure true freedom and peace.

During the next twenty minutes, while Miss Price was getting the dinner prepared to serve us, I was asked very pointedly by Sir Frederick just what was the difference between our Church and its beliefs and those of other faiths. I stated these differences just as directly as he had made his inquiry, without any attempt at explanation or elaboration. Both he and Lady James seemed surprised.

At the close of our evening together, Miss Price requested that our conversation be continued at a later date, saying, "I hope

Mr. Babbel will come again soon so that we may finish our conversation about his religion." At this, Sir Frederick remarked: "The strength of his religion can be seen in the clean, vigorous life which it inspires him to live."

I was pleased that the evening closed on such a pleasant note.

President Alma Sonne, recently appointed President of the European Mission as successor to Elder Ezra Taft Benson of the Council of the Twelve, disembarked at Southampton, England, on Saturday morning, November 16, 1946. He was accompanied by his wife, Leona B., and Elder Wallace Grant Bennett, a missionary assigned to the British Mission. They were met at the docks by President Benson and by President Selvoy J. Boyer of the British Mission.

While passengers for Britain were leaving the ship, President Benson received permission to board it and hold a brief consultation with President Walter Stover, who was assigned to preside over the East German Mission with headquarters in Berlin, Germany. On the ship with President and Sister Stover were eighteen missionaries, some of whom were assigned to work in the French Mission and the others in the Swiss Austrian Mission.

The next Tuesday morning I started my day at 4:30 a.m., working to complete the most necessary items for the visit of Presidents Benson and Sonne to our missions on the Continent. By 11:00 a.m. both presidents were on the bus at the K.L.M. (Dutch) air terminal bound for the airport and then the plane to Holland. President Sonne's last-minute instructions to me were to keep Sister Sonne happy. This was not difficult. Leona B. Sonne was the granddaughter of Richard Ballantyne, who in 1849 started the Sunday School movement in the Salt Lake Valley. She was a delightful conversationalist and a very talented woman.

All arrangements for the travel on the Continent had been completed except for special military orders needed to enter the occupied areas. I was to meet Presidents Benson and Sonne in Paris to work on these orders there and then accompany them to Frankfurt so that I could secure military permission for them to make the trip to Berlin.

By Saturday morning I was in Paris with Presidents Benson and Sonne, who came in on the 7:25 a.m. train from Geneva. But despite the best efforts of the military staff in that city to get some word on permission for us to go to Frankfurt and Berlin, no word was forthcoming. When finally at 12:15 p.m., just 15 minutes before closing time, they were able to contact the captain of the Travel Clearance Section Frankfurt via teletype, he stated definitely that permission to enter could not be granted. It was only by finding the colonel in charge of Western Base Headquarters who was putting on his coat to leave for the day, persuading him to put in a "red-line" phone call to Dr. Olsen in Berlin and Dr. Olsen to do the same to the Frankfurt Clearing Office, that I was able to get the teletyped permission from Frankfurt. By then it was nearly 1 p.m.

Early in the afternoon before our scheduled departure the following day, President Benson invited the French missionaries to meet with us in a special meeting with the district presidents of the French Mission, who had come to Paris for that purpose. It was most interesting to hear their reports All activities were conducted in three languages: English for the benefit of the Americans present, German for the brethren from Strasbourg, and French for the brethren who understood and spoke French.

In Frankfurt a meeting was held with the district presidents of all the districts except Bielefeld. Their reports of the condition of the saints and of the rations they were receiving were most disheartening and caused us deep concern. They were allowed fifteen hundred calories of foodstuffs per day, but actually had only been able to get four hundred to five hundred because in some areas they had not been able to purchase a single item allowed on the ration cards. Meanwhile they were subsisting on mangel-wurzels.

The Germans had had six years of severe rationing from 1933 to 1939 and had suffered even greater stringency of diet during the nearly seven years of war. They had been on a sub-starvation diet ever since the final stages of the war, and it was beginning to take a frightful toll.

At our meeting that evening in the Handwerker Haus, we had a goodly attendance in spite of a terrific downpour of rain. It was saddeningly obvious that the conditions had not been exaggerated to us. The expression on the people's faces was noticeably more haggard and worn than on previous visits. Many of the members seemed just skin and bones. Shaking their hands was almost like shaking hands with a skeleton.

While in Paris I had shipped five CARE packages of foodstuffs to our saints in Poland—the first relief supplies we had been able to send them. I had also sent five packages to families in Germany with whom I had been closely associated before the war. I would gladly have sent hundreds of these packages, but my personal funds wouldn't allow it. The packages sent would have to be my Christmas present to these people.

The military officials we contacted (British, French and American) admitted that the approaching winter would provide the real test. If Europe had a mild winter, the situation in Germany might be tolerable. But if the winter were severe—and every present indication foreshadowed a severe winter—occupation authorities were preparing for real trouble. One estimate had been made that a week of near-zero weather would bring death to 20 percent of the older population, already weakened by insufficient food and inadequate clothing. Another pressing concern was that the discomforts of bad weather would send German technicians out of the U. S. and British Zones into the Russian Zone, where they were being offered extra rations and other inducements.

The following account of Elder Benson's final visit to the missions of Europe is taken from the European Mission History.

> A most successful and pleasant visit to the ten missions of Europe was completed during the past three weeks by President Ezra Taft Benson, President of the European Mission, and his successor, Elder Alma Sonne. Meetings were held with the saints, with the missionaries and mission presidents, as well as with governmental officials and military leaders.
>
> While in Berlin, Presidents Benson and Sonne were dinner guests at the home of Dr. C. Arild Olsen, Chief, Religious Affairs Branch, Office of Military Government for Germany (U. S.). Following dinner, about twenty people, who had been previously invited to the Olsen home, met together to enjoy a two-hour discussion regarding the Church, its doctrines, its organization,

its work in Europe, and some of its distinctive features, such as welfare work, tithing, the Word of Wisdom, the Church missionary system, etc.

In the group were representatives of the Lutheran, Mennonite, Episcopalian, Methodist, Catholic. Quaker, and other religious faiths, as well as members of Dr. Olsen's staff.

Under the blessings of the Lord, the information given was well received. Later, in a brief personal conversation with Dr. Olsen, President Benson related the story of the restoration of the gospel through the Prophet Joseph Smith. Dr. Olsen was not only interested, but expressed his regrets that time had not permitted the presenting of the account of this great event to the combined group He requested the privilege of inviting the group again during a subsequent visit so President Sonne might tell the thrilling story of the restoration of the gospel in this dispensation.

Probably no more fitting tribute can be paid President Benson as he returns to his home than the sincere words of parting expressed by Dr. Olsen in Berlin when he said: "God bless you in the great work you are doing—and I mean it from the bottom of my heart!"[1]

After his return to London, President Benson took the Sonnes, the Boyers and myself as his guests to the Royal Albert Hall to enjoy the music of the London International Orchestra under the direction of Alfred Care. An amusing episode took place there.

As the orchestra was playing Rossini's *William Tell* Overture, I noticed that President Benson's eyes were sparkling as he recognized the theme song for "The Lone Ranger." What happened next was entirely unexpected. As the conductor brought down his baton to conclude this stirring number, and during that brief pause before the thunderous applause which followed, President Benson leaned over to his guests and said in a voice which could be heard for quite a distance, "Hi Ho, Silver, away!"

The time had come for President Benson to return home. The comfort of that journey would be in marked contrast to that of most of the traveling he had done in the previous eleven months. I summarize below his travels as European Mission President

[1]European Mission History, p. 103.

from the time he left Salt Lake City on January 29, 1946, until he arrived back there again on December 13, 1946.

```
By plane  . . . . . . . . . . . . . . . . . . . . . . . . . . . . . . . . . .32,202
By ship and boat  . . . . . . . . . . . . . . . . . . . . . . . . . .1,455
Miscellaneous*  . . . . . . . . . . . . . . . . . . . . . . . . . . .3,405
By train  . . . . . . . . . . . . . . . . . . . . . . . . . . . . . . . . . .9,818
By automobile  . . . . . . . . . . . . . . . . . . . . . . . . . .14,356
Total miles  . . . . . . . . . . . . . . . . . . . . . . . . . . . . . .61,236
```

*Includes UNRRA jeep' and station wagons, buses, street cars, taxis, droshkas, cable railways, etc.

This emergency mission to which President Benson had been called the previous January had resulted in significant accomplishments. Mission presidents were now directing the work in all the missions of Europe except the West German Mission, in which the newly appointed president was soon to arrive. Welfare supplies were moving in orderly fashion and had reached our needy saints in almost all the countries of war-torn Europe. Missionaries were busily engaged in teaching the restored gospel in all of the prewar missions of Europe; and where military restrictions did not yet permit their entry from America, local missionaries had been called to serve full-time and were doing a commendable work. In addition, the gospel was being preached in Finland, which was to become one of the most fruitful fields in Europe.

By the end of the first year we had received and, for the most part, distributed 92 railway carloads of welfare supplies (about 2,000 tons). These consisted of food, clothing, utensils, medical supplies, and a host of sundry items. An active program of shipping individual food parcels, principally from Church members in North America, added tens of thousands of additional critical food and clothing items Some of these items were pilfered in transit, but this loss was relatively small. As well as supplying our needy Church members, we allocated generous amounts of clothing and foodstuffs for use by the local child-care and feeding programs in several countries. In addition, we had been able to secure a number of Swiss military barracks for use in housing many of our refugee saints, primarily from those areas of prewar Germany ceded to Poland and Russia after the war.

Welfare supplies and packages were shipped primarily from the United States and Canada. Distribution was made in Britain, France, the Netherlands, Denmark, Norway, Finland, Poland, Czechoslovakia, Austria, and Germany. Limited shipments were also sent to our members in the Palestine Syrian Mission.

(By the end of March the following year, most of the pressing needs had been met in all of the countries except Germany, Austria, and Poland. This enabled us to divert much needed supplies from our other missions in Europe to those centers still in urgent need. As indicated in chapter 12, just prior to my return home permission was received to make extensive distribution in East Germany, where the situation remained critical.)

On Wednesday, December 11, 1946, I took President and Sister Sonne out to Heathrow airport to see President Benson leave by plane for home. He boarded the Pan American Airways Constellation plane shortly after 4 p.m. I realized that it was wisdom that I remain behind yet a little while. Nevertheless, as his plane roared down the runway after we had waved our last goodbyes, I had an empty feeling that made me wish very much to be with him.

As we drove back to the city, the fog started rolling in.

chapter twelve

The Shape of Things to Come

When we returned to Mission Headquarters after his first European tour, President Sonne stretched out on his bed and said: "Brother Babbel, I feel like resting for about a week. When my head stops swimming, you tell me what happened!"

Then he confided that he had never traveled so far so fast or seen so many people and attended so many meetings in so short a period of time. I agreed to clarify all matters—but one at a time.

(I should mention that one flight required leaving Stockholm, Sweden, early one morning, stopping off in Copenhagen, Denmark, then going on to Amsterdam, Holland, for another stop and ending up in Prague, Czechoslovakia, by 5 p.m. that same evening. Airline officials had said that this was an absolutely impossible schedule to work out, but I had personally checked and rechecked dozens of schedules of all available airlines until I was able to work out a combination of flights by different scheduled airlines that would make such connections possible provided that all flights were precisely on schedule. It did work out, but it was little wonder that President Sonne felt himself to be in a whirl!)

After dinner at the Embassy canteen, we spent a couple of hours discussing future plans regarding the Mission. I was asked my opinion of having Elder Wallace Grant Bennett ultimately replace me. My contacts with him thus far had assured me that he was very capable. The following day President Sonne told him that he was to become my successor if all went well and that he was to learn as much as possible from me about the work.

During our planning session President Sonne expressed admiration for all that had been accomplished by Elder Benson. He assured me that the First Presidency had been most appreciative for the careful detail in our frequent reports and letters to them.

Now that the basic work of reestablishing the missions, getting their records operating on an efficient current basis, and providing the necessary procedures for smooth distribution of welfare supplies had been accomplished, Elder Sonne suggested that a change of emphasis might be in order. He sensed keenly the need to lighten as much as possible the First Presidency's involvement in our day-to-day administrative activities.

Having been a bank president for many years, President Sonne acquainted me with a correspondence procedure that proved to be highly effective during my time with him. He outlined his requirements as follows:

"I will sign no official letter that isn't confined to one page. Is that clear?

"Each letter must be confined to a single clearly identified subject. If we need to treat two or more subjects, you will prepare a separate letter for each subject.

"I will sign no letter that exceeds three paragraphs. You will usually find one or two paragraphs to be adequate."

In the weeks that followed, I inaugurated this practice. If I came to him with a three-paragraph letter, often he would say, "You can do better than that." Then I would shorten it. Results were amazing. We never once failed to get an immediate response to our inquiries. We never had to write a second letter to explain the first one. This practice, in my judgment, was one of the soundest business ideas I had ever encountered.

One evening, President and Sister Sonne, Elder Bennett and myself went to the King's Theater to enjoy George Bernard Shaw's witty play, *Pygmalion.* When we came out of the theater the fog was absolutely impenetrable. With considerable difficulty I finally found our car, which was parked near the theater. I picked up my passengers and began the foolhardy job of trying to inch my way through Hyde Park so as to get to Bayswater

Road—the only straight street leading to Oxford Street and near our home.

I was literally proceeding at a snail's pace. Taxi and bus drivers had long since abandoned their vehicles for the night. People on foot could neither see where they were going nor identify the streets on which they found themselves. I tried walking about twenty feet, but could not see where to go and had to drag one foot along the edge of the curbing to remain on any kind of course.

In spite of these conditions, I decided to keep moving the car as far as possible toward our headquarters. Since they drive on the left in Britain and my steering wheel was on the left side of the car, I was able to open the door slightly, reach out my hand and feel the curbing as I moved along ever so slowly.

By craning my neck out the window opening I could occasionally see the dim outline of the curbing. I could not see the tail lights on stalled cars and buses until our bumpers were practically touching. Often as I passed one of these vehicles, I had to reach out my arm and drag it along the side of the object I was passing until I had cleared it. Then I guided my car back to the curbing.

When we finally got to Marble Arch (the place where missionaries join all the soap-box orators to conduct their street meetings), the buildings were tall enough and the streets narrow enough that I could find my way home with comparative ease.

On entering our home, President Sonne jocularly said: "I can't let you go, not after that wonderful exhibition of driving. I'm sure I shall never find any successor who could equal that performance!" (Drivers and pedestrians alike reported in the newspapers that this was the most dense fog they could recall.)

Since I was the only person in our group who was in possession of valid military permits to all four zones of Austria and Germany, President Sonne suggested that I get my affairs in order and leave for Switzerland to handle welfare matters with the International Red Cross in Geneva and to contact one or more of our key Church leaders in Austria.

The schedule allowed me only one day to prepare. I arose before 6 a.m., brought the mission history up to date, completed a sizeable backlog of correspondence, repaired one of the electric heaters and our radio, installed an inter-office buzzer system and took care of some other miscellaneous items. This all took me until 3:30 a.m.—a rather long day.

Arising at 6 a.m., by 8 a.m. I was on a plane headed for Geneva, Switzerland. As we approached Geneva, we were flying at about four thousand feet above the clouds. The sight of the rugged Alps as we approached Switzerland, with the sun shining upon the glistening snow, was magnificent. Our Swissair pilot commented over the speaker system that he had never seen the view so clear and breathtaking before, so he circled around, banking the plane from side to side so that all the passengers could see it.

Through the fleecy clouds we could see the picturesque Swiss farms and villages nestled among the beautiful valleys, many of which were dotted with deep blue lakes of all sizes. Far in the distance I could see the Bernese Alps, and even beyond to the Tyrolean range in Austria. I'll never forget this sight and the feelings of gratitude that welled up within me as I breathed a prayer of thanks to the Lord for his exquisite creations.

In Geneva I handled welfare matters with dispatch, then boarded an early train for Basel, arriving there just two days before Christmas. We received word that Brother Alois Cziep, district president from Vienna, would meet with us two days after Christmas at the Swiss-Austrian border. I agreed to use my credentials as a means of bringing him into Switzerland overnight so that President Taggart and other mission leaders might be able to visit with him on mission and welfare matters.

I had a pleasant visit with President and Sister Max Zimmer. They were planning to leave for America soon with their daughter Susie, to respond to a call from the First Presidency to assist with the German translation work, which was to be directed from Salt Lake City. I could not imagine anyone better suited or more capable for such an assignment.

President Zimmer through the years has been one of the finest translators I have ever seen in action. When President Benson felt that the time was adequate, he always had Brother Zimmer translate for him, knowing that the final product would be a literary masterpiece. But when his time was short he would ask me to do the job, realizing that at best I would only give an accurate summary of what he wished to convey. Actually my experience as a translator was very limited in comparison with men like Brother Zimmer.

In commenting upon this matter, I could not help recalling a particular job of translating I once did for Elder Richard R. Lyman when he was serving as European Mission President before the war. I was serving as his translator in Leipzig, Germany, in the spring of 1937. It was a cold day and he began by saying, "Many are cold, but few are frozen"—a take-off on the scripture "Many are called, but few are chosen." This usually resulted in a hearty laugh from American audiences.

Realizing that this joke could not be translated into German and still come out funny, I said to the saints in German: "President Lyman has told you a joke that is funny in English. He expects all of you to laugh." They did so. At this, President Lyman put his arm around my shoulder and said, "You're the best translator I've ever had!"

The second day after Christmas, President and Sister Taggart and Brother Niederhauser (district president of the Basel district) joined me to keep our appointment with Brother Cziep at the Austrian border. President Taggart had rented a sturdy used car for the occasion.

Although the day was somewhat overcast, the scenery was indescribably majestic. We entered one valley in which the most intense brilliant blue haze against the mountainside and on the foliage presented a scene of such breathtaking beauty that it all seemed unreal. Our trip through Wallensee was absolutely matchless. The clouds cleared away and revealed the "Sieben Kurfuersten" mountains in all their overpowering splendor. What a glorious sight!

Soon we were near the borders of Liechtenstein—one of the world's smallest principalities. Being so close, we decided to pay this unique place a visit. It is located on the border between Switzerland and Austria. The Rhine river separates it from Switzerland, and the towering Tyrolean Alps separate it from Austria. It is a nation of about eleven thousand people. The guards who met us at the border were venerable old gentlemen dressed in uniforms reminiscent of the Revolutionary War period. Their muskets looked to be of about the same vintage.

After an enjoyable visit we drove to Buchs, the border town through which Austrian visitors must pass. I went to the Canton police at the railway station and with the aid of my passport, military permits, and permanent Swiss visa, was able to receive permission for Brother Cziep, whom we awaited from Austria, to remain overnight with us in Switzerland, provided that I surrender my credentials to the Swiss police as security for his safe return to Austria the following morning. This I was happy to do.

Brother Cziep arrived on time and was overjoyed with our arrangements. We secured comfortable accommodations at a clean hotel, ate a delicious meal—the first good meal Brother Cziep had had for several years—and spent nearly five hours discussing business and mission problems, and also welfare needs in the Austrian section of the mission.

After we had put Brother Cziep aboard his waiting train the next morning, we drove leisurely back to Basel along the steep mountain passes, enraptured with the ever-changing beauty of the scenes before us. Finally President Taggart commented: "Well, Brother Babbel, regardless of how proud we may be of our own scenery in America and no matter how much we brag about it, such scenery as this which we are seeing today slightly excels anything we have to offer for charm, tranquility and sheer loveliness."

The next day, after a refreshing night's sleep on the train, I arrived in Paris and found President and Sister Barker huddled together in a very cold mission home. They and all the missionaries had bad colds. Only three rooms were being heated—and these with small wood-burning stoves. Because of the size of the rooms and the height of the ceilings, even these smaller rooms were quite cold

I spent much of the day in conversation with President Barker discussing various mission problems, several of which I was to refer to President Sonne upon my return to London.

I arrived in London on New Year's Day. President Sonne

greeted me with a note of mock disgust. "That's a fine car you left with us!"

"What's the matter with it?" I asked.

"It won't run," was Brother Sonne's reply.

"Why didn't you have the mechanic come over from the garage and fix it then?" was my next inquiry.

"We did," said President Sonne. "They worked on it for two hours and couldn't get it to start."

"Where are the keys?" was my next question. "Perhaps I can get it started."

"Don't tell me you think you can get it started when the mechanic couldn't fix it?" came the rejoinder.

"I don't know until I try."

With this he gave me the keys. I went into the yard where the car was parked. I tried the starter and noticed that the engine didn't respond as it should. Taking my Swiss officer's pocketknife from my pocket, I pulled down the screwdriver blade and made a simple adjustment on the carburetor.

When I depressed the starter this time it started up immediately and ran as smoothly as always.

I left the motor running to warm it up and went back upstairs to the office. Then I asked President Sonne where he would like to go in the car.

"Don't tell me you got that car started!" He fairly exploded.

"Yes, and it's running fine," was my reply.

"You're not leaving Europe until you train Elder Bennett how to do what you have just done."

"Please don't insist on that," I responded. "Elder Bennett says he isn't the least bit mechanically inclined. But if you will let Sister Sonne come with me, I'll show her just what to do. She's a real handyman."

So began another day. It was a busy one. After supper, Elder Bennett and I joined President Sonne in his office and basked in the joy of learning at his feet. To know him is to know and understand why he is a truly dedicated servant of God.

The bitterly cold weather continued through January. In a

letter to my wife I said:

> This cold spell in Europe has been very hard on many people Some have been frozen to death and unless it lifts soon, the results could be most tragic. Newscasters are carefully avoiding any mention of conditions in Germany, but if this cold spell continues, conditions there will probably become so serious that the military authorities will have to break the silence. I shall be interested during this next visit with Elder Bennett to learn just what the true situation has been during this period.
>
> Sister Sonne has been wearing the heavy wool stockings I brought her from Basel during my last trip and has been most grateful for them.
>
> Strange, isn't it, that when a person has been wandering around taking frequent trips how routine work in the office seems to become. It's quite a chore to write up a thrilling diary episode when in truth all you have done is remain in an office for 14 to 16 hours daily with nothing unusual transpiring. And yet sometimes one can feel the direction of the Spirit of the Lord just as strongly as he does out on the firing line....

On Wednesday, January 15, President and Sister Sonne, Elder Bennett and I left London and passed through Dover en route to Ostend, Belgium. While we were driving through Belgium on the way to Paris, Elder Bennett drove us through Dunkirk, scene of a "miracle" during World War II. As we surveyed the landscape, we saw where the German armies had been poised to annihilate the British troops who were backed against the sea with no apparent route of escape except the sea itself. Between the two armies there had been nothing but gently rolling sand dunes. We came to appreciate the true nature of this "miracle," a fact not normally mentioned in official histories of this heroic action, since this would tend to lessen esteem for the military strategy itself.

The unparalleled valor displayed at Dunkirk has been dramatically portrayed in *The Complete History of World War II*. Following are extracts from the historian's account of what happened;

> For seven days and nights that were almost indistinguishable—days black with the smoke of countless fires that raged not

only in that doomed city, but all along the coast; nights livid with the flashes of explosions and flares and searchlights—uncounted thousands of men proved themselves capable of a heroism to which no words can pay tribute and lived through one of the world's great epics of valor.

Soldiers held their ranks in the streets and at the burning piers, marching without a break to the designated ship when the order was given. Others stood patiently, without complaint, on the bare sand—targets for German bombs and bullets, could any have penetrated the sheet of armor that Britain's fliers kept taut in that great expanse of air—waiting to wade out into the sea and clamber aboard one of the innumerable small boats of every description that had come to their rescue from England. Yachts, cabin cruisers, sport boats, trawlers, fighting boats, tubs whose owners had brought them here to save their fellow countrymen from impending disaster—twelve hundred of these vessels shuttled unendingly back and forth across the Channel between Britain and France. The British sent nine hundred craft. France stood nobly behind her ally: three hundred French ships of the navy and the merchant marine ran back and forth beside the British. Every one of those twelve hundred ships raised anchor only when she was loaded to a weight that would have driven her builders mad with fear.

Endlessly above them roared the protecting planes. Occasionally a German machine would break through the cover, twisting and veering, racing to discharge its missiles. But almost none of those black planes saw base again; those which struck a blow at all were but a minuscule proportion of the horde that tried and failed, smashed and routed by the RAF. The measure of its protection may be gauged by the fact that, of the nine hundred British ships engaged in rescue work all that week, six destroyers and twenty three miscellaneous small vessels were all that Britain lost. Of the three hundred French vessels that sailed beside them, exactly eight were sunk.

Outside Dunkirk the roads were still clogged with troops moving down to the port. Beyond, the Germans were battering relentlessly to storm the city and capture the thousands of Allied soldiers whose one aim was to make the harbor; to escape the hell of Flanders only in order to renew their arms and their strength and return to smash the conquerors. To keep the port safe for them, to keep as open as possible the roads they must take to the sea, other thousands deliberately give their lives.[1]

It seems that as hope was waning among the escaping...an impenetrable fog (like the one we had recently experienced in London) rolled in between the British and German troops. It was so dense and oppressing that for three days the German troops could not move with any of their equipment. During those three days all of the available boats and ships kept cries-crossing the Channel until virtually every single British soldier was able to escape to his homeland before the fog lifted. Thus the Germans found their quarry gone.

President Sonne assured us that this was but another evidence of the Lord's hand in guiding the destiny of nations and of history and should be recognized as the key factor in the "miracle of Dunkirk."

Between January 16 and January 31 I traveled in Belgium, France, Germany, and Switzerland with President Sonne. During this trip President Sonne gave me strict instructions to take what time was necessary, but to introduce him to only four or five key people each day, letting him know of their importance to our efforts and giving him any background information that might be helpful to him in future contacts when I would no longer be with him.

As a result our trip was a leisurely one—a pace to which I was not accustomed, but a pleasant experience nonetheless. We held meetings with civic and military officials, mission presidents, missionaries, local saints and LDS servicemen. All radiated a spirit of good will and genuine understanding, but on this trip no effort was made to initiate any major new projects or plans. It was used chiefly to consolidate gains and achieve an overall orientation of conditions and situations for the purpose of carrying on the work.

During February, at President Sonne's request, Elder Bennett

---

[1]Francis Trevelyan Miller, *The Complete History of World War II* (Chicago: Progress Research Corporation, 1948), pp. 211-212. Used with permission.

and I went to Paris and then into Germany. Elder Sonne was anxious for Elder Bennett to meet the key people, particularly in Germany, and to learn how to handle matters of clearances, transportation, etc.

While in Berlin, we learned that the Russian authorities had finally given permission for our Berlin-stored welfare supplies to be released. These goods were made available to the members in the Russian sector of Berlin only. This resulted in an overwhelming response of gratitude from the Church members affected. But still we had been unable to get permission for our supplies to go to East Germany.

The weather in Germany was extremely cold. We received reports of trainloads of refugees still arriving from the East in freight and cattle cars. Several times hundreds of the passengers had been found frozen to death and their bodies then stacked alongside the railroad tracks like so much cordwood for later removal and burial.

Disease of all kinds was still on the increase. Our welfare supplies were a godsend and were undoubtedly saving many lives.

Near the conclusion of my trip to Germany with Elder Bennett we stopped at Frankfurt. While there I had the distinct and strong impression that, despite our receiving previous assurances to the contrary, no instructions had been given to our contacts in Geneva for shipping welfare supplies into Germany. When we reached Paris I phoned President Sonne and told him of this impression. At his request I proceeded to Geneva to check on this while Elder Bennett returned to London.

When I met with the International Red Cross officials the following day my strong impressions were confirmed. They had not received any instructions from our people in Frankfurt concerning the shipment of welfare supplies. I authorized them to forward shipments without delay to several locations, including Berlin. In view of the continuing cold spell, this was a matter of extreme urgency.

After returning to Paris and completing other business there, I went to Liege, Belgium, to pick up our car and take it back to London. But a check on the Ostend-Dover crossing revealed that ship service had been postponed indefinitely because of large icebergs which had come floating down into the North Sea and the English Channel. One iceberg was spotted nearly three miles in length, twenty-five feet high, and goodness knows how deep. Remembering the fate of the unsinkable Titanic, I could appreciate the concern of the officials, so I arranged to leave by plane from Brussels the following afternoon.

The cold spell continued into March. In many sections of Europe it was reported to be the coldest weather recorded during the previous hundred years. Our work continued as we worked feverishly to provide the much-needed assistance as rapidly and abundantly as possible. Sometimes we were faced with our own discomforts (though nothing like those of the deprived saints in Europe) which provoked comments like the following in a letter to my wife:

> My sniffles still haven't disappeared, but how can they when I sit for hours in a cold, unheated, unlighted office with galoshes to keep my feet warm, a beret to keep my head warm, and President Sonne's sheepskin coat to keep my body warm. Some day I'll laugh at the rigors of this imposed electrical and heating "blackout"...

In the same letter I passed on a useful tip.

> You mentioned in a recent letter how tired you get. President Sonne has the solution. He advises a person to go to sleep for an hour, if necessary, during the middle of the day. He generally does so when he can, with the result that all of his waking hours are alert ones and he gets much more done...

On March 6 the BBC (British Broadcasting Corporation) announced that the cold spell had at last been broken and that the period was now under way which would be known as "The Great Thaw." The following morning they announced that Britain had just received one of the heaviest snowfalls recorded for over fifty years, that hundreds of roads were completely blocked, and that all train traffic between the north and south of England was at a standstill. Strong gales were blowing across the nation; the seas were very rough; and much shipping was imperiled or harbour-locked.

That was our introduction to the so-called "Great Thaw" of Britain. In spite of its severity, for us there was some humor in the situation, as there always is for the layman when the experts are fooled. The circumstances forced us to cancel our intended trip to Brussels.

As an indication of the continuing food shortages, even in Britain, I might mention that for over two weeks Sister Sonne could buy no potatoes. Then one day she stood in a line for forty-five minutes to buy some vegetables. She ended up with three potatoes and two carrots.

On March 14, 1947, President Sonne dictated to Elder Bennett an inclusion for the official European Mission History as follows:

> Elder Frederick W. Babbel, secretary of the European Mission since January 29, 1946, when he and Elder Ezra Taft Benson of the Council of the Twelve left Salt Lake City for London [will depart] for his home via Pan American Clipper with the good wishes of hosts of friends he has made throughout Britain and Europe through his cheerful, unswerving devotion to the Church.

> Not a little of the success which attended the efforts of Elder Benson when he was president of the European Mission was due to Elder Babbel's assistance. Called to act as President Benson's secretary while still in a U. S. Army uniform, Elder Babbel's activities have been directed by the one rule basic in his philosophy—serve the Church, for it is the Kingdom of God on earth.

> He gained a superior knowledge of Germany, its language, people, geography, and customs, when a missionary in the German-Austrian Mission from 1936 to 1939. With this knowledge of Germany he was able to make one of his greatest contributions to President Benson in the work of reestablishing the European Mission and getting relief supplies to thousands of destitute saints in occupied areas.

> He assisted President Benson in reopening missions in France, Switzerland, Holland, Czechoslovakia, Denmark, Norway and Sweden. He was forced to master travel procedures amid chaotic conditions in many places. President Benson traveled over 60,000

miles in 10 months by plane, train, automobile, ship, jeep, truck, bus, and horse and buggy. Most of the time Elder Babbel was at his side—often typing a report to the First Presidency, or an article for the Church News, while on the move. He said that perhaps the worst trip he made was into Poland. Since President Benson's departure December 12, Elder Babbel has been in Germany twice, Austria, Switzerland, France and Belgium.

While this account was ten days premature, it did summarize my activities except for the last week which I have always felt was the culminating event of the entire mission.

Before I left to return home, President Sonne said he felt impressed to give me a special blessing. In it he promised me that I would suffer no serious effects from my experience in Europe and that the Lord would prosper me with vigorous health and strength.

President Sonne had previously expressed some concern because he knew I had traveled among and lived with so many sick and diseased people. On several occasions I had been in areas where the incidence of tuberculosis was as high as 95 percent Many other diseases were also prevalent, but I had only actually suffered from one—a severe attack of ptomaine poisoning after our trip in Poland.

Except for this one setback, I never even had sniffles that turned into a full-fledged cold. I felt that my loss of weight (from my normal 165 pounds down to 117 pounds when the Sonnes arrived) was primarily due to the long hours I had worked—often between eighteen and twenty hours a day and occasionally forty-five hours without sleeping—as well as the many days we had gone without one or more meals. Our four-day fast. in Poland was our longest period without food or water.

It did not occur to me to have a complete physical examination after my return home. It was nearly three years after I had returned home that my good friend Dr. George Taylor insisted upon giving me a complete physical examination. He felt that it was inconceivable for me to have gone through the grueling experiences in Europe without having suffered some ill effects.

When he examined the X-rays of my chest, his concern was vindicated. He discovered that I had calcified spots on both lungs—an indication of my having contracted tuberculosis. I explained that before he prescribed any kind of treatment, I was going to take a few days to claim the blessing President Sonne had given me before I left Europe.

During the next three weeks I was in Rochester, New York. While there I visited the Sacred Grove in nearby Palmyra one Sunday morning. Several inches of snow covered the ground where I knelt to claim my blessing. I felt a wonderful spirit of peace and assurance come over me.

Before I left Rochester I had one of our fine members, a Brother Anderson, who worked as an X-ray technician at the Rochester General Hospital, take some large X-rays of my chest. When I returned to Oregon I turned these over to Dr. Taylor. He was both amazed and pleased to note that my lungs were entirely free of all spots, with no evidence remaining of tuberculosis infection. To this day I enjoy excellent health.

As I neared the end of my mission I had much to reflect on, particularly as regards the magnificent examples of faith and courage I had observed among the European saints. One of the sweetest testimonies that grew out of the total experience was that declared by the devoted men who served as mission presidents during the war years. As they were honorably released to turn over the responsibility to mission presidents from the United States, their testimonies centered around a common theme. "Brother Benson," they said, in effect, "no one can convince us that this is not the Church of Jesus Christ, because during the war years *he was the only One to whom we could turn, and he never once let us down!*"

This was similarly true of other local leaders and members. When I realized how they had had to improvise lesson materials, forego active guidance and encouragement from Church headquarters, and how in some large branches they didn't have so much as a single Bible remaining, the deep meaning of their testimonies was thrilling.

When war was declared in Europe on September 3, 1939, within a matter of hours in some countries and days in others, all missionaries and mission presidents were sent home. In many instances missionaries rather than local brethren had been branch and district presidents and in charge of mission auxiliaries. Overnight therefore most missions were almost entirely stripped of their leadership.

In most missions local brethren who were near at hand were called and set apart to serve as acting mission presidents. They selected local counselors and then undertook the mammoth job of staffing the mission offices and all branches and districts. Just the job of training these members without the benefit of written instructions in their native language would have been a herculean task. Yet there was no time to give them guidelines except, "The Lord bless you and help you until we are able to return."

In the West German Mission the first two acting mission presidents were killed. In the East German Mission, with headquarters in Berlin, Brother Herbert Klopfer—a most capable mission aide was selected as acting mission president. During the latter part of the war he was reported missing on the Russian front. Later it was determined that he had lost his life. Since there were no available brethren in Paris, France, from which to call an acting mission president, a Sister Kleinert was appointed to look after Church affairs there.

Under these circumstances one can understand how totally dependent the leaders were upon the guidance of our Savior and why they could bear such fervent testimony that "He never once let us down!"

In nearly every mission in Europe there were more baptisms during the war years than in a similar period before the war. Some missions had as high as 85 percent of their total membership active. (Finland had 100 percent.) Tithes had increased by as much as 300 percent and fast offerings 600 percent. Yet many areas didn't even have a building in which to hold their meetings.

While many of the major denominations were in a sad state of disarray and plagued with doubts, our saints were full of faith, devotion and gratitude. What a living testimony of the divinity of the latter-day work and of the power of God in the lives of people!

My own testimony, already strong as a result of a previous mission and other Church activities, was further strengthened by the special mission which is the subject of this book. After my return to the United States I had occasion many times to express this testimony in gatherings at which I spoke on the manifestations of the Lord's power during this one-year mission to Europe. Here are some brief excerpts from such a testimony:

"I sometimes feel that we, as Latter-day Saints, don't realize the tremendous *power* that has been given to us as God's children This is not only the power by which the worlds were created but even more important, the power to change men and women and make them gods and goddesses! That's not blasphemy. That's the simple truth. And there's no greater power in all the earth than that which can transform men and women and conform them literally to the image of their Divine Father...

"When the Lord said that his servants 'shall go forth and none shall stay them,' he meant exactly that. The important thing is to be sure that you are one of his servants and that you are doing the things the Lord wants you to do.

"Miracles?...They just seemed to take place almost hourly. There's hardly a thing you can read about in the Old or New Testament but what I have been blessed to see or participate in a parallel experience. I have seen the blind healed, the lame made to walk, the barren blessed to have children. I have seen people at the point of death restored to life. I have seen the power of faith in the lives of men and women and children under some of the most difficult circumstances you can imagine, but the *power of God* was there....

"I witness to you that God lives! I know this as I know that I live. I know that Jesus is the Christ. I shall not know this more surely when I stand in their presence to be judged...I know that God the Eternal Father and Jesus Christ did appear to the boy Prophet, Joseph Smith, because that witness has been given to me and I am under the necessity of bearing that testimony to you. And every time I have the privilege of bearing that testimony, my heart sings because I know that it is the truth....

"I bear this humble testimony to you in the name of Jesus Christ, Amen."

I bore that kind of testimony a quarter of a century ago. I reaffirm it today.

Early on Thursday morning March 20, 1947, President Sonne came into my room and said, "Brother Babbel, I want you to leave right away for Berlin and get permission from the Russians to let us ship our welfare supplies into East Germany. When you accomplish this task, you can go home."

This request came as quite a shock. It was the roughest assignment of all. President Sonne knew that we had already made about a dozen visits on this matter without success. He should also have realized by then that it required several weeks to arrange for necessary military orders, priorities, and plane transportation.—Yet there was something in his manner and request that I could not deny.

Without attempting to make any lengthy explanations or to offer any possible excuses, I decided that, as richly as the Lord had blessed me to that hour, he certainly would not forsake me now. As hurriedly as I could, I packed my overnight bag and left for the airport—without any reservations, priorities, or military papers. This trip would have to be made strictly on the Lord's passport that "they shall go forth and none shall stay them, for I the Lord have commanded them."

At the airport I explained the urgency of this mission and showed the officials my much-used military permits and bulging passport With scarcely a word of protest they accepted these credentials and issued me a round-trip ticket; and I was on my way to Berlin.

The flight was pleasant and without incident. At Berlin I had to do some tall explaining, but the military officials accepted my explanations without question. Then I hurried to the military headquarters to get the necessary clearances. They quickly obliged.

It was early afternoon when I phoned the Russian headquarters for an appointment to talk with them about permission for the shipment of welfare supplies into East Germany. They invited me to come right over. When I entered, I was quite surprised to see that the Russian general in charge was there with some of his aides. Since he spoke German at least as well as myself, we entered into our discussion without delay

After about an hour (it seemed much longer) of my explaining the purposes and programs for making food, clothing, and medical supplies available to he Church members in East Germany we reached a point where I held my breath awaiting the general's decision. I didn't have long to wait. His answer was "Nyet"—No!

I was praying as earnestly as I knew how. Somehow I felt that this could not be the final answer. President Sonne had not sent me here to fail. And hadn't I felt the Spirit of the Lord with me richly as I made my explanations and requests to this group? Fur a moment I did not know what to say. Then I received a flash of inspiration. I continued the conversation in the way I felt guided to do. In essence I said:

"General (calling him by name), I am grateful to you for granting me this privilege of discussing this vital matter with you. I sincerely respect you and realize that you must have good and valid reasons for giving me the answer you have Just given me.

"But if you will be as frank and honest with me as I have been with you, you must at least acknowledge that I have told you the truth in these matters. We have no ulterior motives, we are only interested in helping to keep some of these critically needy people alive; and we don't care who gets the credit."

There was a noticeable pause. The general looked at me intently. Then he said with a smile: "I must admit that you have been extremely frank and honest with us…and because you have been, we are happy to grant you permission!"

My heart was overflowing with gratitude as I witnessed the power of the Lord change *no* to *yes*. I thanked the general and shook his hand warmly. It did not seem wise to be effusive in my appreciation. As I left the room my entire soul cried out in gratitude to my Heavenly Father. And I truly felt that now my mission in Europe was finished.

The next day I returned to the European Mission office. After greeting me, President Sonne asked, "Did you get permission from the Russians?"

"Yes," I replied.

He smiled at me with a radiance that I shall never forget. "I knew that you would enjoy the power of the Lord in getting permission," he said. "Your mission is now complete. You may go home as you have planned."

Then we sat down and I related to him what had taken place since I left him the day before. We discussed the several items I had handled, and particularly the Russian permission. He was pleased. But most of all he looked as though a heavy weight had been lifted from his heart. Through eyes filled with tears we both expressed our realization that this was the Lord's culminating witness to us that those called as his servants who put their trust in him as they truly seek to do his will have the promise:

> *And they shall go forth and none shall stay them, for*
> *I the Lord have commanded them.*

Index